Family Words

Books by Paul Dickson

Think Tanks

The Great American Ice Cream Book

The Future of the Workplace

The Electronic Battlefield

The Mature Person's Guide to Kites, Yoyos, Frisbees
and Other Childlike Diversions

Out of This World: American Space Photography

The Future File

Chow: A Cook's Tour of Military Food

The Official Rules

The Official Explanations

Toasts

Words

There Are Alligators in the Sewers
and Other American Credos

Jokes

Names

On Our Own: A Declaration of Independence
for the Self-Employed

The Library in America

Dickson's Dictionary of Baseball

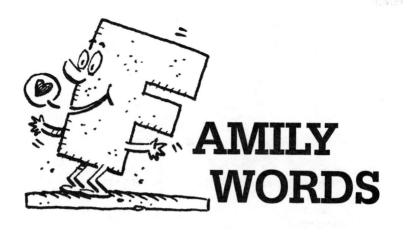

AMILY WORDS

The Dictionary for People Who Don't Know a Frone from a Brinkle

Paul Dickson

Addison-Wesley Publishing Company, Inc.

Reading, Massachusetts   Menlo Park, California

New York   Don Mills, Ontario   Wokingham, England

Amsterdam   Bonn   Sydney   Singapore   Tokyo

Madrid   San Juan

Library of Congress Cataloging-in-Publication Data

Dickson, Paul.
  Family words: the dictionary for people who don't know a frone
from a brinkle / Paul Dickson.
    p.   cm.
  Bibliography: p.
  ISBN 0-201-15593-1
  1. Family—United States—Language (New words, slang, etc.)—
Dictionaries. 2. Words, New—English—Dictionaries. 3. English
language—United States—Slang—Dictionaries. 4. Americanisms—
Dictionaries. 5. Communication in the family—United States—
Dictionaries. I. Title.
PE3727.F35D5 1988   88-14496
427'.973—dc19   CIP

Original illustrations by Ellwood H. Smith
Cover design by Ellwood H. Smith
Text design by Joyce C. Weston
Set in 10-point Serifa by Compset, Inc., Beverly, MA

ABCDEFGHIJ-BA-898

First printing, August 1988

Family expressions are the poetry of everyday life.
—Steven J. Zeitlin, Amy J. Kotkin, and
Holly Cutting Baker in *A Celebration
of American Family Folklore*

Your family, like every other family, has a language of its own, consisting of unintelligible catch phrases, favourite but not generally known, quotations, obscure allusions, and well-tried, but not intrinsically humorous family jokes.
—A.A. Milne's "Christmas Party" in
*A Table Near the Band and Other
Stories*

Family varieties of a language are liable to cause exasperation to the uninitiated, especially those who marry into a family that has developed its own linguistic habits.
—G.L. Brook in *Varieties of English*

... children blundering among the syntactic blunders offer a delight that perfection itself would never yield.
—A.E. Coppard in the foreword to his
tale *The Man from Kilsheelan*

To—whom else?—my family.

Introduction

PHLURGG is a word that I have never been able to get out of my head. It got in there about 1947, when I was still in grade school, and came out of the pages of a long-gone magazine called *1000 Jokes,* which used to feature a comic almanac carrying "Lunar Phases, Weather, Prophecies and Phlurgg." It did and still does mean something to me; to wit, "important miscellany, a better class of et cetera, that which is too important to throw away." There is, as I write this, a phlurgg pile on my desk within a foot of my elbow, which I will eventually drop into a bulging file folder labeled Phlurgg. There is a box in the tool room for hard phlurgg and a mug on my dresser for pocket phlurgg.

Phlurgg is on its way to becoming a bona fide family word, a linguistic curiosity in that it is only understood by a very small circle, and when you say that word outside the family or small group of friends, others don't know what you're talking about. More often than not, family words can be traced back to a kid or a grandparent, and sometimes they get passed down from generation to generation. They seldom escape the province of one family or a small cluster of families—so are therefore seldom written down and must be gathered in conversation. Bear in mind that these are not words that clever people sit down and create just for the sheer fun and challenge of having created them, but rather they just pop out of the fabric of a family or a small group of people. They can't be forced because they work to fill a gap—a place where there is no real word or the real word doesn't work.

For several years now I have been collecting them. I collect them for the simple reason that I find them fascinating to hear and repeat and think about. Also, because of their ephemeral nature, there is a certain challenge in building such a collection that, I can brag, could emerge as the definitive assemblage of family words.

The thing that got me started on all of this was an article that first appeared in *American Speech* in 1962 called "Family Words in English." It was written by the great lexicographer and lover of American language Allen Walker Read who, after giving some charming examples, admits that individually such words are of small use to the lexicographer. But then he adds: "Nevertheless, such material should be watched by the lexicologist for its value in showing tendencies in the language. The family is the matrix in which we see the bubbling up of linguistic experimentation. One of the greatest gifts that can come to a speaker of a language is the freedom to move about among the possible patterns that the language provides for him. This feeling of 'at-home-ness' develops and flowers in the family circle."

But it is clear that Read enjoys the examples themselves—the actual "effervescing of language" as he refers to it—rather than generalizing about them. One that he seems to have liked particularly was a royal family word recorded by the present Queen of England's former nanny Marion Crawford in the book *The Little Princesses.* The word is *hoosh-mi.* She wrote, "*Hoosh-mi* is a pleasant word made up by [Princess] Margaret for the nursery mixture of chopped meat, potato, and gravy, all '*hoosh-mied*' up together and spoon-fed to its victim. Later the word was to become a part of the schoolroom vocabulary and a mix of any kind was always known as *hoosh-mi*."

Despite Read's seminally important article, there was little new interest in the phenomenon until 1974, when the Smithsonian's Office of Folklife Programs began collecting family folklore in the form of stories, customs, photography, and words and expressions.

The Smithsonian showed that family expressions are as important as single words, and in its publication *Family Folklore* are examples like *jumping off the fifteenth-story window for a breeze on a hot day,* which, in one family, meant to overdo. Read had pointed out earlier that many family words are, in fact, family alphabetical abbreviations or acronyms. The one he uses to illustrate is F.H.B. for Family Hold Back, which is used to let the family know that an article of food is in short supply and to hold back so that the guests will have enough. This, of course, presumes that the guests have never heard the F.H.B. injunction before. Read says that this is one of the rare family words that long ago broke into general use. In fact, he recalled using it when he was a child and notes that Eric Partridge dated it back to the middle of the nineteenth century. F.H.B. is just the start, and there are a number of other coded dinner-table messages, including:

F.L.O. Family Lay Off. This is pronounced flo and is used by families that realize most of their guests already know what F.H.B. stands for.

M.I.K. More In Kitchen. This indicates that which there is plenty more of. It is another abbreviation like F.H.B. that has entered the language.

M.Y.O.B. Mind Your Own Business. This has become

3

as popular as F.H.B., but less well known is M.Y.O.P. for Mind Your Own Plate, which is used when, for instance, one child is stealing french fries from another. M.Y.M. in a Philadelphia family is used at restaurants and other people's dinner tables for Mind Your Manners.

More of these dinnertime initialisms appear shortly in the main dictionary that follows. Before presenting that dictionary, however, let me tell you how the collection was put together. A large number of words and expressions came to me in letters from people who read my book *Words*, in which I announced my interest in starting such a collection.

Another large block of examples came as a result of radio call-in shows. On January 24, 1982, I appeared on a talk show on WIND in Chicago. From that time and up to March 29, 1988, when I appeared on a talk show on WRC in Washington, D.C., I have been able to get myself invited onto more than forty call-in shows, and I have been on the air in places ranging from San Francisco to Boston to Miami to Saskatoon. Typically, on such shows, family words are discussed for a few minutes, and then the call-in lines are opened up and people call in their favorite examples. It seems to touch a nerve because in almost every case, there were more calls than there was time to handle them. A number of shows invited me back, and, in fact, I have appeared on two popular San Francisco talk shows, each on a different station, more than a dozen times.

If nothing else, these shows helped the collection become geographically diverse. The only drawback is that the call-in format does not allow for last names, so I've been unable to credit many valued contributions properly. Lacking a name, entries collected in this manner carry the call letters of the station. The

4

locations of the stations are at the end of the book in the master list of acknowledgments.

I have also gotten words as a result of a half-dozen speeches I made on the topic, including talks before the Maryland Library Association, the American Translators Association, the Weld, Maine Historical Society, and the 1984 Wonderful World of Words Conference. Some fine examples came as a result of an essay I did on the subject for National Public Radio's "All Things Considered." Still others came from an article on my quest by Richard Lederer which appeared in a number of New England newspapers that carry his fine "Looking at Language" column. Walter Berkov, emeritus book editor of the Cleveland *Plain Dealer*, solicited family words in a series of columns for that newspaper and generously allowed me to borrow from his collection. By far the largest single haul came after I wrote a small article on the subject for *Games* magazine, in which I asked for additional examples from readers. More than 800 letters—811 to be exact—were sent to the magazine, which published a few of the best examples. All the rest of the letters were turned over to me for use in this book.

Last but not least I relied on friends, family, and acquaintances to supply me with even more examples.

Through this process I have collected more than 3,000 words and phrases and have come up with five main conclusions about them:

1. Some people have family words that are, in fact, unbeknownst to them, archaic dialect or mainstream words that have long fallen from popular use. This is remarkable in that they are still alive as vestiges of the past: true verbal antiques. The first example of such a word appears in the dictionary as *croodle*.

A column on language that was sent to me from *The Listener*, a New Zealand magazine, contained the following question from a reader: "For four generations my family have used the word '*beezle*' with the meaning 'to annoy, to harass, to bedevil'—'I was thoroughly beezled from being continually interrupted.' We cannot find the word in a dictionary; is it purely a family expression?"

The answer given by Ian Gorden, the author of the language column, reads in part: "*Beezle* was once part of the standard language and it then retreated to the dialects, from which it has in turn all but disappeared. I am delighted to find that it is alive and well . . ." Gorden adds that a related form of the word lives on in *embezzle*.

2. Some people have family words that are actually popular everyday words but don't realize it. A lady in the Sun Belt reports that her family calls the room outside the kitchen the *mud room*, while a man of Irish ancestry reports that his family uses the word *gonif* for a thief. The woman was amazed to learn that mud rooms are common in the Frost Belt, and the man was taken aback to learn that *gonif* was a common Yiddish word. *Church key*, for beer-can opener, was offered by a man of the pop-top generation who did not realize that the term was common slang in the not-too-distant past.

3. Some of the words have begun the process of moving out of the province of one family or small group to a larger and more geographically diverse group of people as they are reported independently in various parts of the country. The aforementioned M.I.K. and F.H.B. (which, among other things, was the subject of a 1985 Erma Bombeck column entitled

"Mother Makes Decision, Puts FHB Plan in Action")
are good examples of this, and another is the entry
daw-daw. They are hardly "proper" words as yet, but
they are beginning the trek into the mainstream.
Wayback, as the name for the cargo section of a station wagon, was reported by a number of families.
The author of a 1963 article in *Woman's Day* on words
remarked on the originality of a child using "trash" as
a verb ("I trashed it," said Mac happily), with no in-
kling that the word would come into its own in the
age of protest and be applied to things like plate
glass windows.

These terms fly in the face of an assumption made
in big letters in an ad for the *Oxford English
Dictionary* that appeared in the summer of 1985 in the
New York Times Book Review. The ad said of that un-
rivaled dictionary, "If it's not here, it ain't English."
What the ad should have said was, "If it ain't here, it
ain't yet come to the attention of this dictionary's
editors."

**4. It is all but impossible to find a family that does
not have at least one family word, although it may
take a member of that family a while to recall which
words or phrases are the family's own.** This final
conclusion is not my own, but one first made in 1923
by Eric Partridge in his book *Slang Today and Yesterday* and borne out during my collecting of family
words. Partridge, who referred to family words collectively as family slang, wrote, "All families, if they are
more than a mere collocation of related individuals, if
they meet often together, and especially if they prefer
their own company to that of others, have their own
private slang; some few an extensive vocabulary,
most a score or a dozen or even fewer words and
phrases."

For what it is worth, a number of people submitted a dozen or more examples in their letters, and one woman, Gayle Grove of Hagerstown, Maryland, offered forty-two examples from her family.

5. Family words are not limited to a mere word or short phrase, but may take other forms. One example drives home the point: "Because one of our family members has a hearing problem, we use some sign language," writes Laura Bobbitt of Arlington, Virginia. "There are some family signs that have come into use, but are difficult to explain. One, however, may amuse you, and doesn't depend on standard sign language." The gesture involves putting your hand in front of your face and repeatedly moving your fingers up a quarter of an inch and down a quarter of an inch. "That's a microwave."

Enough preambling. Here are some of my favorites. Most are true family words collected firsthand from the family or families that use them. I have also taken the liberty of including a handful of deliberate coinages that are not true family words but creations that work so well that I couldn't resist adding them. To keep them apart, the few deliberate coinages appear in boldface type.

— ACKAZOOMA —

Abediah! Cry that goes up in a family when one family member interrupts another. Marjorie Hunt, of McLean, Virginia, traces the cry back to a peddler in the Missouri Ozarks who was periodically invited to her father's house. There Abediah would "talk forever and interrupt everyone at the table." (Quoted in *A Celebration of American Family Folklore.*)

Accafortis. Anything that is especially strong in flavor, taste, or muscular ability is "stronger than accafortis" in the family of Kenneth P. Weinkauf of Athens, Ohio. Nobody in the family knows what it means.

Accumulata. Jean Scott Creighton of Bath, Maine, reports that this word is "derived from 'accumulate' and makes a handy noun to describe that sort of family junk that no one can seem to get rid of or that piles up in attics and cellars. I thought it was a word and have used it for ages, but I can't find it in *Webster's Unabridged* (mine anyway). I inserted it as a trial in my first novel and the copy editor let

9

it stand, so either I've gotten away with something or it is a legitimate word."

Ackazooma. The threatening stem protruding from the core of an apple. From Frank Whitby of Littleton, Colorado, who says, "As I was sure that the ackazooma *had* to be removed *before* eating, I was unprepared for a world full of ackazooma-intact apple-eaters when I reached the age of seven years. Thus, the tradition of ackazooma removal before eating an apple has continued into my adulthood."

Acrosters. Those people who insist on mispronouncing words, e.g., *acrost* for across and *eck setera* for et cetera. (Minnesota Public Radio)

Afterbearers. Term created and used as a logical antonym to forebearers. (WRC)

Agida. A nervous stomach or heartburn, brought on by agitation. Radio personality Joel Spivak, WRC, Washington, D.C., recalls it as a neighborhood word from his childhood.

The term is enjoying an ever-widening circulation, and it has even been used in Woody Allen's *Broadway Danny Rose*, in which a character complains of "agida in the panza." The etymology of the word was discussed in the "Word Watch" column in the June, 1987, issue of *Atlantic* magazine: "Professor Luigi Ballerini, of the Department of Italian at New York University, believes that *agita*, an Italian-American word, comes from the Italian *acidita*, a technical term meaning acidity."

Ahh-hees. The uncomfortable feeling produced by putting on a bathing suit that is still damp. Reported by Laurie Travis of Nashville, who adds, "The immediate reaction of the wearer is to shiver and say Ahh-hee, ahh-hee."

Ahhstick. The doctor's tongue depressor in one Virginia family. (WRC)

Air-raid. One family uses this as a code word warning of an attack of what air-raid suggests when spelled backwards.

Alligator. Jawlike device used for removing staples. (KMOX)

The Alligator Blinks. From the Barouch family of Flushing, New York, this expression is used when something seems unbelievable but is really true. A letter from the family gives the etymology:

"This expression came about in Florida when we were vacationing. Not far from our hotel was a motel called something like 'Gatorland Motel' and it had a huge concrete alligator with jaws agape out front (this was actually the entrance to the motel, you had to walk through the jaws). When we first passed it our daughter was very impressed. We passed it again several times during the vacation, but the next time that we had passed it our daughter had asked us why the eyes were no longer blinking. Now to us these 'eyes' looked like just concrete spheres set into the rest of the concrete alligator. . . . Every time after that when we passed this statue she complained that the eyes were not blinking. . . . Finally we passed the alligator one evening (as we must have the first time) and saw that there actually was a light set up inside the 'eyes' that blinked on and off when it was dark out. There was no indication of this during the day. We were very surprised and more than a little apologetic to our daughter (who was very proud to have stuck to her guns and be proven correct—she was only four) about not believing her."

AL Sauce. Steak sauce in a Seattle family. They began to use it when a child misread the label on a bottle of A-1 Steak Sauce.

Altravert. Person of wild mood swings from introvert to extrovert. (KMOX)

Ambisinistrous. The opposite of ambidextrous, for a person who is clumsy with both hands—two left hands. Reported by a surgeon who says it came out of the operating room and has now entered his family. (KNBR)

Amn't. Contraction of *am* + *not*. Cynthia MacGregor of New York City says that she has been using it since childhood. She has also been complaining that it is not an acceptable English word, which, of course, it should be.

Analalia. The improper mixing of languages as in "blu cheese." Joe Turner of Vista, California, hunted in vain for a word for this and finally invented his own.

Anhinga. Something dreadful. From an incident in which a bird-loving family member spotted an uncommon bird, the snakebird or anhinga, and another exclaimed in mock horror, "Oh no, the mysterious and deadly Anhinga!" (Tom Gill)

Annie-wumps. Stumps of flooded trees, usually in advanced states of decay. Created by the family of Jeremy Burr of Bridgton, Maine, and used in canoeing.

Anony. [a-non-e] The unseen person responsible for domestic troubles; Mr. Nobody. It came from a child's attempt to grasp the concept and word *anonymous*.

Antelope Picture. Any snapshot, the subject of which must be explained or pointed out. From Carolyn Chappell of Arlington, Texas, who says it came from snapshots of antelope in Wyoming in which the animals appeared as amorphous dots on the horizon.

Antook. One Chicago woman proudly brought home an "antique" brick. The dealer told her it was used to keep people on sleigh rides warm after it had been heated. Her family created the word to describe both the brick and other dubious antiques. (WHDH)

Ants. In at least one family this is what those flecks of chocolate are called in which ice cream cones are sometimes dipped. Other more conventional terms for them are shots, jimmies, sprinkles, and, according to one source, in England they are known as "hundreds and thousands."

Apads-bratwil. An elaborate family acronym in the Dunn household of Lakewood, Ohio, used when it is time to wash the dishes. It stands for Always Put Away Dry Stuff Before Rinsing And Tackling Whatever Is Left. (Russell J. Dunn, Sr.)

Applaudience. An audience that has come to applaud: specifically, those composed of parents and grandparents at children's piano and dance recitals. Presumably the term was created to reassure a child who is nervous about "all those people" who would be at his recital. (WRC) See also *Living Room Quality.*

Armentrude. A mythical proper name (for William Q. Armentrude), a noun "Armentrudism," and a verb "to armentrude," this word came into being and died with the Washington *Star.* It deserves presentation. Armentrude was the man who fought red tape in the bureaucracy by boring from within with mischievously dumb regulations. Thus, "He armentruded a new set of rules making it illegal to collect used cat food cans."

Quoting from a *Star* editorial of December 4, 1976,

we are told, "It was Armentrude, in a brief stint at the Department of Agriculture, who advised egg farmers in Rule 88: 'Do not attempt to fry eggs in their shells.' Discovered and sent packing, he alighted briefly at the Department of Commerce, but only long enough to write the inspired Rule 104 of the Office of Washing Machine and Dryer Administration: 'It is not necessary to remove buttons to wash a shirt.'" His greatest work may have been for the Occupational Safety and Health Administration, where his set of rules for the use of stepladders contained the classic injunction, "When ascending or descending, the user should face the ladder."

The *Star* is gone but Armentrudism goes on.

Armlace. Necklace worn on the arm and an improvement on "bracelet." Created by the nephew of E. Goodman of University Heights, Ohio.

Arping. The practice of trying to read a record while it is playing. (KGO)

Arson. A coincidence in the family of Mindy Kettner of Edmonton, Alberta. Ms. Kettner explains, "When explaining the word 'coincidence' to his six-year-old daughter, Dad used the example of a church which had recently burned down in our town. He said that if a second church burned down, it would be a coincidence. The six-year-old looked up at him and said, 'Or arson.' 'Arson' has meant 'coincidence' in our family ever since."

Arther. Thermometer, as in "our ther(mom-eter)." (Barbara Gilfillen, Hamilton, Mass.)

Aspergantis. For close to twenty years now a sign at the Greenlawn Cemetery in Jacksonville, Florida, has read "Beware The Aspergantis." According to an Associated Press item, the sign has been a major factor in reducing vandalism at the cemetery.

Atsifice. A second-choice substitute. "This started," says Carole L. Carrick of Newark, Delaware, "when my little brother (then aged four or five) asked for a glass of chocolate milk, which wasn't available. My mother asked, 'How about a glass of milk, will that suffice?' My brother looked doubtful, and asked, 'What's atsifice?'

Asyou. The bottom or top step of the stairs where things are put—from "As you go up/down take this with you." (Faith M. Thompson, Claremore, Okla.)

Atomic Upsweep. See *Pompies.*

Aunt Vi's Piano. Any piece of furniture, wall, or room decorated with an inartistically arranged excess of family memorabilia. (Marion Lehuta, Montgomery, Ala.)

Auttoben. A hair color that *ought to have been* on a dog. From Sharon A. Harris of Lewiston, Maine, who says, "My father used to describe my hair with that word meaning a cross between auburn and ash."

Awaks. To confuse the public through open debate. From the AWACS (Airborne Warning and Control System) and the prolonged technical debate attending it. "The Star Wars debate is becoming awaksed." (WAMU)

— BACKWASH —

Back Wash. Refers to the question asked when kids share a glass or bottle of soda pop. "Are you sure there's no back wash?" It refers to spit that may have slid back into the drink. (Mr. and Mrs. Mark Petersen, Brockport, N.Y.)

Bacon Alert. Smoke detector. (Laura Bobbitt, Arlington, Va.) Also, *Dinner Detector* and *Meatloaf Alarm*.

Bacronym. An acronym in which the word was chosen to fit the letters. Created by Meredith G. Williams of Potomac, Maryland, to cover the likes of GEORGE (Georgetown Environmentalists Organized against Rats, Garbage, and Emissions) and NOISE (Neighbors Opposed to Irritating Sound Emissions). The oldest and best example in Mr. Williams's collection is SURFSIDE (Small Unified Reactor Facility with Systems for Isotopes, Desalting, and Electricity), which was a project of the New York State Atomic and Space Development Authority announced in 1970.

Bagaduce. Fancy family name for outhouse, now

used for any trip to the "facilities." From Esther S. Gross of Waldoboro, Maine, who got it from her father, who said "I'm going to Bagaduce" when questioned about where he was going when he left the house at night. (The state of Maine has a Bagaduce River, which may or may not have something to do with this family word.)

Balkin. Chicken. Paul B. Clifford, Godfrey, Illinois, writes, "Our youngest daughter when aged three arrived at this name for chicken because her daddy would imitate chickens by crowing balk-balk-balk, etc."

Banana. One couple, Martin and Charlotte Gardner, always use this when they say goodbye, or even goodnight. According to Martin Gardner, "This evolved as follows. We started saying *hasta mañana*, which slowly evolved into *hasta banana*, and finally just plain banana."

Bark. Crust on bread, as in "I'll eat it if you cut the bark off." (Vickie Moreland)

Barkative. The creation of a ten-year-old in the Mende family in Ontario. It is a perfectly logical term for dogs that bark a lot.

Basemess. Basement. (Nel Gibbs, Schofield, Wis.)

Ba'shower. That taken by children making the transition from bath to shower; a shower taken with the plug in. (KMOX)

B.C.S. Big Corporate Stuff. Says Sherry Reardon of Delray Beach, Florida, ". . . what my husband goes to work in the morning to do. Originally he did B.M.S., Big Management Stuff, but now that he's not a manager any more he does B.C.S."

BCT. Boring Clerical Task. Used in the "office family" of Wendy Heldke of Milwaukee to give a modicum of dignity to dull work.

Bealed. Swollen or abscessed. From Anne Higgins of Sharon, Pennsylvania, who adds that it is one of those words from western Pennsylvania that don't show up in the dictionary. It is used in such lines as, "I have a bealed finger."

Beamish. A bit depressed, as in "I'm feeling beamish today" or "You're looking rather beamish." From British writer Russell Ash, who adds that it supposedly means "shining brightly" (and is used that way by Lewis Carroll in his *Jabberwocky*) and notes that there is a village called Bemish in northeast England. It is applied to the blues in his family because "it just sounds right."

Beanwhistle. A term of endearment in my family. Who knows how or why it started.

Bedjudsky. A knuckle pinch in at least one neighborhood. (CFQC)

Benble. Any minor anomaly—sweater pills, for instance. (Cate Pfeifer, Milwaukee, Wis.)

Bender. Elbow in the Fosse family of Mendocino, California.

Berry Bugs. Books (pronounced like "bugs" by a child) taken from the "li-berry." (Sher Bird Garfield, Seattle, Wash.)

Bevabovits. Creatures that keep kids awake at night, mess up rooms and such. (CFOS)

BH's. Buffalo horns, which are those little curls of hair that won't lay down. (Mary Tanner, Weatherford, Tex.)

Biasm Chasm. A brainless handsome man among the female members of a Washington, D.C., family. Or, as one of them puts it, "A male dizz ball." (WRC)

Bibble. Loose sole on a tennis shoe or sneaker, from the sound made by flipping your bottom lip with your finger. (Donna Hargrave, Vancouver, Wash.)

Bibsy. A little flighty or irresponsible. A word used by author Agnes Sligh Turnbull and first reported in 1948 in the magazine *Word Study*.

Big Grandma. That grandmother who lives farther away than "little grandma." (Scott Newsome, Richmond, Va.) *Far Nana* is used in another family. (Mary Little, Dedham, Mass.)

Bip. A North Carolina woman said her daughter created this word for the kind of person who buttons the top button of a sports shirt and wears black socks to a picnic. (WIOD)

Bird Feet. How your feet feel and look after you've been on a ladder for a long time, or have had your feet on the rungs of a stool; curled over, turned under, feet. (Jane Tesh, Mount Airy, N.C.)

Biscuit. When someone in the family does something right, this word is called out. It started with a family dog that was given a biscuit when it did a trick. (Toni Blair, Orange Park, Fla.)

Biz. Defecation. Many families have a word like this left over from toilet training days (*happy toads*, for instance), but what is significant here is that the lady who reported it, Adrian B. James of San Pedro, California, added, "I was shocked by the naming of a laundry detergent Biz . . ."

Bizark. A portmanteau word combining *berserk* and *bizarre*, which means eccentrically frenzied. It comes from Philip N. Price of Brooks, Maine, who got it from his Aunt Margaret.

Blap Cloth. Fabric diaper in a family who calls the disposable versions just plain diapers. "You'd better put a blap cloth under her chin because she's drooling." (This appeared in a 1983 column in the *Boston Globe* on grandmothering.)

Bleeper. A common word from the childhood of Howard Channing of Clear Lake, Washington. He explains, "The kids I played with used to chase each other and try to press a finger on a mole, a wart, a pimple, or any skin blemish and say 'bleep-bleep.' The blemishes were bleepers."

Blesper. The cotton or wool stuffing that occasionally comes out of upholstered furniture. From Larry Broadmore of San Fernando, California, who says of it, "I have no idea where the name came from—but this substance was to me like 'the blood' of the furniture, and therefore very important and mysterious."

Bloviate. A word made popular by President Warren G. Harding. It would appear that he began using it in public about 1920. A paragraph in Samuel Hopkins Adams's book, *The Incredible Era,* eloquently displays the word: "Harding loved to make speeches; to go out and 'bloviate' as he called it. But his type of verbose and overornamented oratory was becoming outmoded. To turn him loose upon a public grown critical of ponderous clichés would be too risky."

The creation of the word has been widely attributed to Harding; however, Francis Russell's biography, *The Shadow of Blooming Grove: Warren G. Harding in His Time*, calls it "a word then current in Ohio, but long since obsolete" and goes on to say that it meant "to loaf about and talk and enjoy oneself."

It was no fluke that this particular president gave it currency. Roger Butterfield claimed in *The American Past* that Harding "was an expert at wrapping a single idea in several thousand pompous words." The late Charles McCabe loved the word, and on November 9, 1972, he devoted his entire San Francisco *Chronicle* column to it. Among others, he made this point: "Bloviation perfectly described the windy gasbag that' Harding was, and that he knew he was. Like many another politician, Harding seemed to derive some deep physical relief from public speaking. It was rather like a good bowel movement."

After Harding's death, it still found its way into print in contexts that did not refer to the president. In a 1953 article in *Saturday Review* by Stanley Walker, writer and lecturer Robert St. John is described as a "trend-setter, journalist and bloviator." In 1953 a Missouri newspaper talked of Texas politicians who "bloviated far into the night." It made it into *Webster's Seventh New Collegiate Dictionary*, first published in 1967, but was dropped from the next edition. It was defined, "to orate verbosely and windily." But it still lives on, with the most recent example occurring in *National Review*, September 12, 1986, in an article in which conservatives bloviate.

Harding is also credited with giving the world the word *normalcy*, making him a linguistic pioneer among first executives. However, there seems to be more to the story. Quoting again from *The Shadow of Blooming Grove*: "Harding did not coin 'normalcy' although he did bring it into common use. It first appeared in 1857 in Davies & Peck's *Mathematical Dictionary*. Indeed reporters claimed that Harding did not even revive the word, that in his script he had written 'not nostrums, but normality.' In reading the speech he mispronounced this as 'normaliticy,' to the concealed amusement of reporters who were later kind enough to change the gaffe to 'normalcy' in their copy."

Blowers. Tableware not used during a meal that can be put back in the drawer or cupboard without

21

being washed. From Pam Herman of Centreville, Virginia, who says, "I suppose it started from saying they only needed to be blown off rather than cleaned."

Blurge. A blinding gust of snow. It comes from Johnathan R. Hancock of Syracuse, New York, who tells how it was created by his father:

"While driving the family back and forth to Turin, N.Y., on ski weekends, he attempted to quiet the rowdy passengers by telling scary stories. One dealt with a phenomenon called the 'blurge,' a dense gust of snow that bursts over a snowdrift and across the road. In his story, cars entered blurges never to appear again."

Blutz. According to Joanne Lee, who reported it, *blutz* "is a verb which describes putting one's open mouth on the partially submerged anatomy (any part that's big enough will do) in a swimming pool (or a bathtub if *it's* big enough) with lips held slackly and sort of blowing to produce bubbles, or at least a lot of water activity and noise. The action can be accompanied by a humming sound if one is able to do it. It's pronounced in such a way as *not* to rhyme with *clutz* . . . but more like the 'u' in the color blue. A guy I was in love with when I was thirteen or fourteen used to do it to me all the time (whenever we were in the water together). I don't recall it was particularly erotic, but it sure felt nice." Other contributors offer *blubberslatch*, *broop*, *phlurrt*, and *bubblekiss* for the act of blowing on a baby's belly. See also *Zerbert*.

Boby. A very small animal of any type. From Eileen Mozingo, who reports, "My daughter, when a toddler, spied a puppy and told us that it was so small, it was a boby. She (and we) have since used the term to mean any small animal—a boby horse, a boby rabbit, etc."

Boggy. A child's plump belly. (KGO)

Boik. From "Best Of Its Kind" and used as a noun, adjective, and verb. From James H. Harms of Quechee, Vermont, who said it was common to his high school forty years ago. John A. Main has long used B.A.T. for "Best Available Technology," and O.O.A.K. for "One Of A Kind."

Boleo. Belly button. "My two sisters and I were born in the middle 1940s," writes Carolin Winslow of Newburg, Pennsylvania. "I think [boleo] derived from the fact that when our mother bought oleo, it came in a plastic bag, with an orange dye button in the center. One produced a nice yellow oleo by squeezing the oleo and dye together in the bag. To us, the dye button looked like a navel."

Boljolls. Any vague sort of ailment. From writer Martin Gardner, who reports that this word and the companion *humpfloggins* were used by his grandmother and adapted by the rest of the family. He is not sure if they are family inventions or old expressions from Kentucky, but has never found either in a slang dictionary.

Boogoeaster. Child's rendition of ego-booster. (WIND)

Borv. The small V formed by short hair at the nape of the neck. (Tina Stano, Brookline, Mass.)

Boscalotus. [bosk-a-lot-us] An all-purpose word in my family used mostly by my father, especially when he was in a jolly mood. It was at once something you said to an infant, an answer to the question of what was for dinner, and an exclamation of the same genre as "Eureka!" and "Great balls of fire!"

My father picked it up as a boy when he heard it from an Italian greengrocer in his neighborhood. It took him a while to figure out that the man was saying "box of lettuce."

Bow-tiesed. "When our two boys were baptized," writes Patricia J. Axline of Challis, Indiana, "they, for the first time, wore little suits complete with bow ties. When asked where they had been by a neighbor, one replied, 'to be bow-tiesed.' This has come to be used by our family to describe being formally attired."

Boyhatten. Nonalcoholic drink for a generation of boys who would be too embarrassed to order a Shirley Temple. (WCKY)

Bread Picks. The little flat plastic clips placed on the ends of bread wrappers to keep them twisted shut. (Peter DeWeese, Fairfax, Va.)

Breck-a-fuss. The space between two pushed-together twin beds. Submitted by Karen Lane of Merritt Island, Florida, who says it was coined by a friend's father who complained that the space was dangerous and that one could fall in and *brack a foos,* which is Yiddish for break a foot.

Brinkles. The marks on your face from the sheets, couch, or whatever when you wake up. (Mary Rogers, Madison, Wis.) See also *Revlacormia.*

Broo. The singular of bruise; the cross between one bruise and a boo-boo. (Roberta Sandrin, Derwood, Md.)

Budabuda. The inside of the lower lip, so called because it is used in conjunction with forefinger to make the sound "budabuda." (WIND)

Bunab. An object that is worthless or has no discernible use. The word and this meaning were given as a family word by a caller to a Washington radio station (WRC) who said that his father had once been sent a bunab, identified as such, by a friend many years ago.

It is quite possible that bunab has the same meaning in other families, due to the tireless efforts of the late Al Crowder of Mason City, Iowa. Crowder and his bunabs merit a digression at this point.

Crowder, who died in 1981 at the age of seventy-seven, was a musician, inventor, radio personality, and music store proprietor. But his greatest mark came as the spokesman for an imaginary company known as Orville K. Snav and Associates. It was a marvelous spoof that lasted for years, beginning on a fateful day in the 1950s when Crowder produced his first BunaB (which he always wrote with a capital B at either end). He had discovered a box of empty clarinet reed cases and decided to do something with them. What he did was place two pieces of taped-together insulated wire—one red and one blue—in each case, which he embossed in gold with the words, "Genuine, Improved, #7 BunaB." It came with a sheet of instructions that, among other things, said the BunaB would "with reasonable care, give years of trouble-free service. It has been scientifically inspected and checked against the master model at the factory." At the bottom of the sheet it was announced that the BunaB was the product of Orville K. Snav and Associates.

Each #7 was accompanied with a registration card that, when filled out and returned, was rewarded with a rambling letter from Crowder, which might tell about Snav's brooding ever since he was again passed over for a Nobel Prize or about the two-month-long New Year's Eve party still going on at Snav Tower. Often he would sign off with the line, "Our Mr. Snav would like you to have dinner together next time he is in town," but at other times he would note that Snav had not been seen in public since "the incident in Peoria."

And there were other BunaB's, including:

BunaB #2. Zurdick. A small game, replete with playing board and pieces, encased in a plastic box with the notice TOTALLY UNPLAYABLE, NO MAT-

TER HOW MANY TIMES YOU READ THE IN-STRUCTIONS. All correspondence from Snav Tower was stamped *Don't Play Zurdick With Strangers.* (This stamp appears on a 1982 letter to the author, sent after Crowder's death by his widow Louise, who signed herself Minerva P. Snav.)

BunaB #3. "The Man's Between Shave Lotion" to be applied between applications of before and after shave. It was a seemingly empty plastic bottle whose contents could be reconstituted by adding water.

BunaB #4. A small, high-precision dial that adheres to any flat surface and turns from "off" to "on" again.

BunaB #5. The first record to be played while watching television. It is completely blank.

BunaB #6. The only difference between #6 and #7 is their similarity.

In addition, the Snav group also manufactured PMM (Post Meridian Morning) Shields, black half-circles to be pasted over the left side of a clock to obliterate what Crowder called "one of the anathemas of modern civilization—the morning."

But it was the original #7 that got all the attention and netted Crowder a modicum of national attention, including four appearances by Crowder on the Garry Moore television show and a profile in *Playboy,* which said of the object, "It does nothing—physically, that is. But psychologically, it's as miraculous as digital computers or any of the complex gadgets, of real or dubious import, that crowd our ulcerous machine civilization. Its devotees look upon it as a tiny, clear Bronx cheer aimed at our mechanized age, a parody of rampant technology and its highly touted advantages."

Before it was over, some 40,000 #7's were shipped from Snav Tower; all sorts of people had put in their orders. H. R. Haldeman even bought one for Richard Nixon. Every one of the original Mercury Astronauts had them, and the late Dave Garroway bought them in lots of a dozen to be used to see if a person could be trusted (if they didn't think they were funny, they were not to be trusted). Jimmy Carter returned one that was sent to him by Garroway.

All of which goes to say that BunaB (with two capital B's) is a word and a concept that should never be forgotten. Nor should Crowder's line, recalled by his friend Patricia Samson, uttered when postal rates went to thirteen cents: "That's ten cents for postage and three cents for storage." Sampson said of him, "He had a mind like a Chinese fire-cracker going off . . ."

Bunce. The heel of a loaf of bread. It is from a lady whose family has used the term for almost sixty years and who was in her twenties when she first heard someone call a bunce a heel. She says, "*Heel* is a terrible word for the most delicious part of the loaf, the bunce." Apparently others agree that *heel* is a bad word for this part of the bread, since it is called the *truna* in one family and the *tumpee* in another. (WIND and WRC) Todd W. Wallingen of Beaver Dam, Wisconsin, calls it a *canust,* which rhymes with "the roost."

Bunkies. Family password giving one permission to sample something that another family member is eating. (Arlene Yolles, Westport, Conn.)

Burtie. Signal that one's fly is open. From an Indiana family that got the idea from an old man in the neighborhood named Burtie who was never properly zipped up. (WIND) See also *X.Y.Z.*

Busque. To quote directly from the man reporting it, "When you are eating dinner and the dog puts his nose on the window; what is left on the window is busque." (KGO)

B.W.K. Initialism for Burglar With Key. Announced loudly by a parent or grown child when entering the other's house through a locked door, as reassurance that it *really is* a family member. (Robert G. Chamberlain, San Marino, Cal.)

— CAROLOGIC —

Cachunger. Machine for credit card charging, from the noise it makes. (Kim Haglund, Taipei, Taiwan) Not to be confused with a *chencha,* which is what several families call the remote television channel selector.

Carologic. Bizarre, illogical reasoning. From a Wisconsin woman, Debbie Paliagas, who says it came from the many strange explanations dreamed up by her sister Carol. "She explained in perfect carologic that saltshakers have holes so the salt can breathe."

Catchie-wotchies. Catch-all name for second class hors d'oeuvres, such as canned peanuts, plain crackers, and popcorn. Shrimp and brie are not in the catchie-wotchies category. (WRC)

Catsmile. A forced and phoney smile, such as those produced when a person is asked for an opinion about an expensive new dress or suit that looks awful. (WRC)

Cement Pond. [sea-ment] The swimming pool in the old "Beverly Hillbillies" television show and the preferred name in one northern California household. (KNBR)

Charlie Lagow. Verb for letting dishes soak in water overnight (in order to get out of washing them right after a meal), as in, "Let's Charlie Lagow those dishes 'til later." From Rebecca Rasor Freeman of Rockwall, Texas, who says that the term goes back a few generations to the name of a man known for his laziness.

Chenga. See *Chencha*, under *Cachunger*, above.

Cherklet. To put on conversational airs in the presence of company. According to Felicia Volkman of Coral Springs, Florida, the term originated when a family member, a New Yorker by birth, was watching her r's too carefully when she offered visitors some "cherklet."

Chibbles. Stuff, as in "pick up your chibbles." From Edward Mayo of Kennebunkport, Maine, who got it from his wife's family, who used it for a long time.

Chik-chik. Cutting finger and toenails, as in, "Here, let Mommy chik-chik your nails." (Geri Kirkpatrick, Wiarton, Ont.)

Child-cheater. Rubber spatula used to clean the frosting bowl so well that there is none left for the kids to lick. (Carolyn Gray, San Bruno, Cal.) Another family called it a *kid cheater*. (KMOX)

China Clippers. Synonym for dentures. (KMOX)

Chipslunch. The crusty, greasy remains in a frying pan after you cook hamburgers for lunch or dinner, often used in an abstract adjectival form, as in "What a chipslunchlike day." (WIND)

Chizzly. *Chilly* + *Drizzly*. A particular kind of day. (WIND) This blend word is one of many that have followed in the path of *smog* (smoke + smog). Others submitted as family blendings: *sneet* (snow + sleet), *smust* (smoke + dust), *snoud* (snow + low clouds), *mugid* (muggy + humid), *gusterly* (gusts + blustery, for strong, undifferentiated winds), *grismal* (an awful time: grisly + dismal), *drizzable* (drizzling + miserable), *chippy* (chilly + nippy), and *blerzo* (from below zero).

Just how far you can go with this was demonstrated in an essay by John Allen May in the *Christian Science Monitor* back in 1953. After discussing *smog* and *smaze,* he writes,

"But there is also fmoke, which is a mixture that has more fog than smoke, and hoke, which has more haze. Furthermore, through inversions there may be frequent days of goms and ezams, ekomf and ekoh.

"There is smist, which is smoke and mist, and misoke, which is mist and smoke. There is smulphog dihazeide and there is tarfog monsulphide and so forth."

All of this got started with *smog*, which first appeared in print in 1905 and is attributed to a Dr. Des Voeux, the first president of the British National Smoke Abatement Society. See also *Snirt.*

Chopity, or Chop-chop. A sublime level of comfort and coziness; for example, nestling in for an hour with a beer, book, and comforter. "I'm leaving work and am determined to have a chopity evening." (Ann Cuniff, Chicago)

Christmas Adam. The twenty-third of December; the day before Christmas Eve, so called because Adam came before Eve. Created by an opportunistic child looking for a reason to open a gift two days before Christmas. (Karen Cukrowski, New Haven, Conn.)

Chronism. The opposite of anachronism, a creation of William Safire in his *New York Times* column. Chronisms, according to Safire, are "words quivering in the aspic of time, perfect for use by dramatists who want to give historical scenes the flavor of authenticity, starring Vera Similitude, my 1940s *heartthrob.*"

Safire gave a number of examples, including milk

bottle, slide rule, pals, atomic (replaced by nuclear), dime store, nightclub, corset, phonograph, and smut peddler (now porno dealer).

There are more: ice box for refrigerator, car wreck (or "totaled" the car) for automobile accident, Victrola for phonograph (never mind hi fi or stereo), swamp for wetlands, junior college for community college, grocery store for supermarket, and shopping center for mall.

Cirvagerous. Extremely large. "Would you do me a cirvagerous favor?" (KGO)

Clara. Nobody in the family involved can recall why, but this is what is said when a man's trousers or woman's slacks are strategically stuck in the wrong place. (WCKY) In one group at the University of Wisconsin, this phenomenon of cheek-stuck pants is called a *wedgie.*

Clarty. The state of being hot and bothered that comes at the end of a hard day, as in "Your father's a bit clarty tonight." (WRC)

Clinker. Word used in place of a dirty word. "Did your brother actually call you that?" "He used a clinker but I knew what he meant." (Carol Andresen)

Clunk-waa. A child falling out of bed. From Soo Bishop of Forsheda, Sweden, who adds, "My husband and I coined this after having two children, because the sounds so accurately describe the incident."

Coffee. Snow that has aged and become tan. From coffee ice cream, which it resembles. (Caroline Bryan)

Common Sewer. Anything that stinks but is also expensive (perfume, after-shave lotion, tobacco, etc.). The term came from a highly aromatic tobacco blend that was labeled "Connoisseur" by the tobacconist. (J.G. Timm, McGregor, Tex.)

Con. Main dish discovered one night in the Brown family of Utica, New York. The kids wanted chili con carne, but neither chili nor meat could be found, and so a dish was created with the remaining ingredients. (Marilyn Brown)

Conclusory. An adjective formed by the blend of *conclusion* + *illusory* and applicable, for instance, when one makes an allegation that seems based on the facts but is not.

What makes this term unusual is that it was announced as a new word in a footnote to a court decision. According to an article in the September 14, 1987, issue of *Insight* magazine, it appeared in a decision of the Wyoming Supreme Court by Justice Walter C. Urbigkit, Jr., who wrote, "After painstaking deliberation, we have decided that we like the word 'conclusory' and we are distressed by its omission from the English language."

Concrachener. The string that hangs from a single light bulb. (Libby James, Greeley, Col.)

Confectionate. Sweetly affectionate. (Barbara Calures)

Conushelled. The condition a kindergartner's papers are in when they are brought home; the wrinkled look that young children bring to things.

This word was reported on John Gormley's radio show on CFQC in Saskatoon, Saskatchewan. Several days later, he wrote, "As it turns out, a linguistics professor friend tells me the word is derived from a German word spelled *knutschen*, which means 'to crumple.' He says this could possibly be crossed with *knish*, which means 'to gnash.' Derived from all of this is the way our professor friend would spell the word the caller used. It is *knuschelt*."

Coo-coo. Flatulence. Reported by Garrett Riggs, who says it came from a mother's "'scuse oo"—baby talk for "excuse you"—whenever the tot would pass gas. "The closest the child could come to imitating her sound was 'coo-coo,' which has remained in the family dialect," says Riggs.

Coogie. [koo-jee] Any niche for storage that is too low to stand up in, such as either end of an attic or an upstairs room where the ceiling slopes down to the floor. (Sylvia Blowers, Mancelona, Mich.)

COOOO-KIE. Delivered in the manner of the Cookie Monster on "Sesame Street" to mean: here is your food, dinner is served, or have a bite. (Janet W. Crampton)

Co-parents. A word hatched to describe all the parents shared by a married couple. It originally appeared in a letter to *American Speech* in February, 1927, and underscores the point that the quest for names for groups within families is not new (see, for example, *Niblings*). The original letter to *American Speech,* from Cyrena Van Syckel and Henry W. Toll, also suggested *parimutuals* and *couplancestors* for co-parents.

Copilunch. Dinner on the stove that is exactly what the spouse just walking in the door had for lunch. (WRC)

Cornflakes and a Hard-boiled Egg. Used to cheer up someone who is not feeling well, this phrase is usually expressed as "What you need is cornflakes and a hard-boiled egg." Reported by Ross Reader of Hampshire, England, who got it from a neighbor. It dates back to a relative who broke his jaw in a car accident. The jaw was wired, and he could only eat what could be sucked up through a straw. The next morning he was brought the aforementioned combination for breakfast.

Cortsty. An endearment meaning cute, lovable. (Stephen V. Masse, Amherst, Mass.)

Cotton Broom. Mop. (Evelyn Bowles, Edwardsville, Ill.)

Couldja House. Any tumble-down, usually rural, house that appears unfit for human habitation. "The term comes from the question, 'Couldja love me enough to live in it?' asked years ago of an aunt by her husband, who buys, repairs, and sells such dwellings" writes Sue King of Raleigh, North Carolina.

Crackanoodles. Uncooked pasta. (WCKY)

Crackenflash. Ersatz swearword. (WRC) There are many such words reported, including one from a woman who still uses an expression adopted by her parents from a fictional family. It is Pa Foyle's "God in Brooklyn," from Christopher Morley's *Kitty Foyle.* Then there is *Holy ol' Red Rattlin'*, which Dawn Hogarth of Derry, New Hampshire, picked up from her grandfather.

Crinkles. Popcorn hulls that stick in your teeth. (KNBR)

Cronk. To knee someone in the back of the knee, usually causing the victim to stumble. This came from the Bronx childhood of a San Francisco man, who still gets the urge to cronk his co-workers but usually resists it. (KGO)

Croodle. To nestle against someone else for affection and warmth, as a child will do when being read to. This word and its meaning came from a caller to a St. Louis radio station, who probably had no idea that the word was listed in Ernest J. Barlough's *Archaicon* as the author discovered later. *Archaicon* is a collection of bygone words and phrases. Barlough even found *croodle* in print in Charles Kingsley's 1857 novel *Two Years After*, in which the heroine "clung croodling" to the hero.

Crouton. An insult word, used in a family in which

the parents were very strict about the kids not using words like "jerk" and "dummy." *Dipthong* was also used. (Cate Pfeifer, Milwaukee, Wis.)

Crucials. Plastic pants put over a diaper. Writes Lisa Freedman of Bellevue, Washington, "My mother always referred to plastic pants as crucials—because they were. My father never knew that they were called anything else until one day, sometime during the fifth child, he was sent to the store to buy more. To his embarrassment he found out that no one knew what 'crucials' were, and he discovered the real name for this required article of clothing."

Crummy Buttons. Stand-in curse word that attracted national attention in early 1987 when the Deputy Police Chief of Brunswick, Maine, Richard Mears, suggested it to his rank-and-file as a substitute for common four-letter words.

Crumping. The act of putting something together at the last minute.

Crunch. The place to which things disappear; a place of which you have no knowledge or understanding; never-never land. "The word came about," says Martin M. Bruce, "when my infant son, in the midst of being bathed in a bathtub, inquired 'where does the water go?' I explained the incoming route from reservoir to tap, then into the tub, out the drain, and out to the crunch."

Crytearian. Child who cries with the slightest provocation. It was probably the creation of a radio personality named Uncle Don (actor Don Carney) who used it on his WOR (New York) kids' radio show in the 1940s.

(The compiler of this dictionary carried this word with him since first hearing it, and still cannot think or read the word "criterion" without thinking "cry baby." Blind luck was at work when I was looking something up in an April, 1946, copy of *Word Study* and found a small list of Uncle Don-isms for kids that not only included crytearian but *romeroff, fakerup, scuffyheeler, borrowmanian, leavearounder, muddlerup,* and *nevergiver.* The short article noted, "Any youngster within WOR's seven-state listening area can tell you what these words mean, or, if you don't tire easily, you can dope them out yourself.")

Cumpishion. Pincushion. From Warren R. Johnston, whose daughter, Jennifer, created it at age two. It survives as a preferred alternative.

Cutter. All-purpose word for that which cannot be found. "Where's my cutter?" in this Maryland home meant a fork, a hat, a letter, or anything else that was missing. (WRC)

C.Y.B.T. Short for Can You Believe This! Uttered in one family as a means of dealing with such things as returning from a shopping trip having forgotten to buy the item that got you to go shopping in the first place. (Russell J. Dunn, Sr.)

C.Y.K. This stands for Consider Yourself Kissed. It was given to me by a woman whose father was a germ-conscious doctor who always said C.Y.K. to the kids when he put them to bed during the cold season.

— DADS —

Dads. Any one of the four corners of a rectangular cake that, of course, contain more icing. It has been in one family's vocabulary for at least two generations, and it may have come from a father who preferred corners. Now it is often used as a cry— "Dads!"—by a child claiming the corner piece. (KNBR)

Daffodil. Margaret Atwood of Bloomfield, Connecticut, defines this one as "A rather silly female with '40s makeup on a '50s face, rhinestone-studded glasses' frames. . . . Her car has a dreadful plastic flower on its antenna, so she can find it in the supermarket parking lot, often a daffodil. Prototype spotted by my son, age seven, many years ago."

Darfish. To speak German, from the kids in a household whose sole link with their German-speaking elders was the line "Darf ich aufstehen?" (May I leave the table?) (Caroline Bryan)

Daw-daw. The tube of cardboard inside a roll of toilet paper, but only after the paper is gone. It was reported by Frank Brusca of Woodstock, Maryland, in response to my essay on family words read over the air on the "All Things Considered" radio show. In

38

response, a Colorado woman wrote to say that it was hardly original, as it was used in her family, too, and a Missouri woman insisted that it was a "Dawda-Dawda" in her family. *To-do To-do, Doot-do, Taw Taw* and *Der Der* were reported from Missouri, Pennsylvania, Ontario, and Vermont. However, the greatest disagreement came from two listeners who said that it was not the right word. Quoting Kevin Dammen of Fargo, North Dakota, "It is named after its usage. It is a musical instrument and is played by placing it to the mouth and uttering its real name, 'HOO-HOO.' Also, the huge tubes you find during the holidays from gift wrap are called, corresponding to their size, 'HOO-HOO-HOO's.'" A Maryland woman, Leila Shapiro, reports that it is a HOO-HOO in her family, too. Kathleen Quastler of San Diego says it is neither: "Every one knows it's a *drit-drit*—has been for years!" *Foomer* works for the Dick family of Corvallis, Oregon.

Debutantrum. A society girl in a snit. Recalled by writer Don Crinklaw of St. Louis, who gives this background on the word: "I think I am the only one of my place and time, not to mention height, weight, and physiognomy, who remembers a forties' humorist who called himself Colonel Stoopnagle. I remember that he authored a book of humorous observation that I used to take out of the Marshalltown Public Library all the time. The one sequence I recall from the heart of the text was a catalog of necessary but heretofore uninvented inventions, and the only one of those I remember was an eleven-foot pole for touching people you wouldn't touch with a ten-foot pole. The part I *do* remember was an odd little dictionary at the back of the book." Crinklaw not only recalled *debutantrum*, but also *champagnezee*—a gentleman who makes a monkey of himself in a nightclub; *fagtory*—where they make cigarettes; and *dadpole*—a papa pollywog.

Dee Dee. Cinnamon and sugar mix used to sprinkle on toast. The word comes from Diane Curtis of Covina, California, who says it came from a TV chef who always said "dee dee dee dee" while sprinkling spices on a dish.

Didit. Raised highway lane markers that make the sound "didit, didit" when you ride over them. (KGO)

Diggy. Butter. This term becomes self-explanatory when one sees this family's butter dish. (J.L. Fosse, Mendocino, Cal.)

Dingbats. All breakfast cereals. An oddity because, according to the man who reported it, the term "stems from a dream which a family member had, about a new breakfast cereal called Dingbats Flakes. In the dream, there was a picture of Archie Bunker on the cereal box." (Tom Gill)

Dip Hat. A person who insists on driving very slowly on a highway, so-called because nine out of ten of these people wear a dip hat (fedora). (Sue Mosher, Port Williams, N. S.)

Disgusto Slot. Too narrow space between kitchen fixtures (such as between a refrigerator and a stove) where utensils fall and succumb to years of grunge. (Linda Kent, Cambridge, Mass.)

Dishonest Tie. Clip-on bow tie. From William Amatruda, whose uncle came up with the term.

Disirregardless. A word that involves a double grammatical error, close to a swearword in the family of Nancy Craig of New Hope, Pennsylvania.

Disneyland Daddy. Divorced father who occasionally visits the kids and shows them a good time. (Susan Mills, Three Rivers, Cal.)

D.I.T.D.W.C. [dit-dwack] An abbreviated initialism for

"Are the dishes in the dishwasher clean?" (Robert G. Chamberlain, San Marino, Cal.)

Do. The thicker part of soup—meat, potatoes, and such. (KARN)

Dobrydurus. Temporary state of stupidity; confusion. "I had just woken up and had a moment of dobrydurus." (WMCA)

Doka. A running toilet. The word is used both to describe the phenomenon and as a call for someone to jiggle the toilet handle so that the noise will stop. (KMBZ)

Do-less. State of lassitude. Anne Higgins of Sharon, Pennsylvania, is the reporter: "My mother-in-law sometimes described herself as feeling 'do-less' (she didn't feel like doing much that day)."

Dorgis. A royal family word that appears in Graham and Heather Fisher's *The Life and Times of Elizabeth II*. Dorgis are "the result of a romantic interlude involving one of the Queen's corgis and a dachshund belonging to Princess Margaret."

Dotsia. The name for any plant whose name you don't know. *Coleander* is a synonym for dotsia. These are not to be confused with *Horsephlox,* which is the name of a flower you don't know the name of. (WIOD) Then there is the *Spendidium* for flashier flowers and plants. See also *Nearsturtiums* and *Farsturtiums*.

Drapins. Drapes and curtains as a class. From Fran Urban of Parma Heights, Ohio, who picked it up from her nephew Jeff.

Drasual. Clothing appropriate to occasions that are neither dressy nor casual. (Christina Jones, Winthrop, Me.)

Dreal. To melt down the sides, as a scoop of ice cream does when placed on hot apple pie. From Ruth R. Wedge of Georgetown, Maine, who now accepts it as a Scrabble word.

41

Drippings. Things left behind by houseguests, such as dripping bathing suits and cameras. This is from Dale and Barbara Pullen of McLean, Virginia, who have been known to leave drippings.

Drut. Timothy B. Messick of Rome, New York, reports, "In the school where I teach a 'drut' has long been a student whose ability in academics is far surpassed by his aggravating and annoying habits." It can be spelled backwards.

Dtz. [ditz] Little Christmas gift, a stocking item, often a small, cheap wind-up toy. (Dave Carr, Owen Sound, Ont.)

Dufferish. Something a duffer would do or say. (Gene Deitch)

Dugan. As in "doing a Dugan," it refers to a decisive action that is suddenly given up with a return to one's original state in worse condition than one started. Named for a family that sold their house in New England and then moved to Idaho, only to return to their original town a few weeks later after they couldn't find work. They had to buy a worse house for more than they got for the original. (Jean Scott Creighton)

Dumbsquat. A numbskull. This was reported by several people who preferred it to other names of its type because, as one of them put it, it carries well when shouted out of a car window at another driver.

Dupert. "This is our family's word for a backrest consisting of two pieces of hinged wood, supported by two cords, which sits on the floor for watching TV &c.," reports Nelson Hanke of Garfield, Arkansas.

Dups and Dovers. Meals made from refrigerator cleanings (warmed-*ups* and lef(t)*d-overs*). (Dorothy LiaBraaten, Minneapolis, Minn.)

— EEKSER —

Eaper. Any object without an obvious function, such as the kind of thing one is likely to find at the bottom of a box at a rummage sale. (KMOX)

Eardo. Condition of a dog's floppy ear when it is flipped backwards. (Dorothy J. Martin, Kalamazoo, Mich.)

E.B. Crude initialism for "exposed booger." In use in a large family for years, to tip its members to this social transgression in coded lines like, "You'll never guess who I bumped into last week, E.B." (Anon.) See also *One Over Par.*

E.E.'s. Large breasts. The woman who reported it said it was a word she had heard as a child and was used by her mother and her aunts. Only when she became an adult did she realize that it was probably a reference to the two E-cups of a large bra. (KGO)

Eekser. The lever on an ice cube tray, so-called because of the noise it makes when pulled. (KMOX)

8377. A Canadian woman said that she and her brothers were not allowed to say the word *hell* around the house so they said "8377," which "sort of" looked like the word "hell." (CFQC) (A man whose boyhood was spent in Connecticut in the 1920s remembers "7734" as serving the same purpose—it looks like *hell* upside down and backwards. It is especially well suited to the angular numbers of electronic calculators. His wife adds that a popular expression at her church-connected college in Pennsylvania in the 1940s was "H-E-Double-hockey-stick.")

Emboggle. To become mired in confusion. Reported by several families. It is interesting that in 1952 the then-Secretary of Defense Robert A. Lovett introduced this same word to describe the situation in which one general says the situation is white, and a second general says it is black. The result is a state of embogglement. (From a Sept. 3, 1952, article in the *Christian Science Monitor*)

E.M.F.H. Every Man For Himself. Call made on those evenings when, according to Christine H. Tiffany of Memphis, Tennessee, ". . . Mom doesn't feel like cooking and the family must fend for themselves."

Epiconstituent. That which is clearly self-evident or obvious. Often used in adverbial form for something that is "*epiconstituently* true." (Nona West Eudy, Cleveland, Oh.)

Evatea. Anything that is unbearably strong, especially coffee, tea, or alcoholic drinks.

Sent by Mike Wilson, who explained it in a letter written May 25, 1984. "I submit this in memory of my grandmother, Eva Wilson, who died just last night! It seemed that whenever my grandmother would make tea, it would be so *strong* that one

44

would have to wait to drink it, waiting as the liquid oozed down the glass."

Evidentually. Blend of "evident" and "eventually" for that which is not now evident but will be eventually. (WRC)

Expud. Not nice, rejected (usually applied to food). This is part of the family vocabulary of author Meredith Starr quoted in Eric Partridge's *Slang Today and Yesterday*. Other words collected from the Starr family include *droomers* for bedroom slippers, *flimmick*, "to throw away," and *miffy* for stale (of food gone moldy).

~ FECSH ~

Fact. Al Williams of Atlanta reports, "Growing up a twin, my family often had to hear the same story from my brother unbeknownst that I had already told it. In order to be tactful, when one of us would begin such a story, the other would simply say 'fact' and that got everyone off the hook."

FAFA. [fah-fah] Paternal grandfather, that is, FAther's FAther. FAMO [fah-moo] is FAther's MOther. (Lisa Simon Jablon, Randallstown, Md.)

Faff. To move about and look busy, but get nothing done. "It was a good morning for faffing." (KNBR)

Fannyfriend. Verb used to describe the action of a male dog pseudo-interacting with a sofa, blanket, pillow, leg, etc. To mount, as in "Willy is fanny-friending the blanket"; or simply "Willy is fanny-friending." From James Thorpe, III, who is not sure if it was invented by his daughter Elizabeth at age three or his wife Diantha, to explain what the dog was doing.

Fant. To act like an infant. "Stop fanting" would be a proper admonition to a seventeen-year-old behaving immaturely. (WRC)

Fardo. The embarrassment you feel for somebody else. "Fardo takes place," says the man who reported it, "when a man drops the end of his tie in the soup at a dinner party and can't figure out how to get it out without dripping soup all over the place." (KGO)

Fash. To work too long over something; to fuss rather than finish. Author Agnes Sligh Turnbull wrote in *Word Study*, October 1948, that this was an old and archaic Scotch word that had currency in her family. She added that the old Scotch version of the Bible contained the line 'Dinna fash yersel because of evil doers,' which appeared in the King James version as, "Fret not thyself because of evil doers."

Fecsh. A spontaneous burst of warm feeling expressed in an eccentric manner. Example (spoken dramatically with a wild light in the eyes): "I want to hug you so tight your guts come out." From the word *affection*. (Sharman Badgett, Goleta, Cal.)

Feebly. A bit of food or other foreign material on one's face. From Margo B. Schworm of White River Junction, Vermont, who traces its family origin, "Somebody once read a story in which a character was described as having 'a feebly growing down on his face.'"

Fidufa. Pile-driver. This from Denis Norden on the BBC show "My Word."

Fifty-one AR. A liar. Explained by Mavis Koehler of Long Beach, California, "When we were kids we were never allowed to be impolite and rudely call someone a liar, so we got around it by calling them 'a fifty-one AR.' Fifty in Roman numerals is, of course, L . . ."

50 psi. Airhead—from the average pressure of a bicycle tire. (Jim and Jule Michelini, Okinawa)

Filet de frying pan. Depression-era euphemism for hash. (Joseph C. Goulden)

Filmin. Doris L. Pertz of Pine Brook, New Jersey, wrote, "My brother used "filmin" for film as a little boy, and the family held on to it. ('Did you put filmin?' and 'Did you get filmin?' [an extension]). Filmin is a noun."

Finector Snout. All-purpose part name. "Hook 'er up to the finector snout and she'll be ready to roll."

Fingerpots. The places where the fingers join the hand. After a melting orange sherbet cone was cleaned up, a young man informed his mother that she had cleaned his face and hands but missed his fingerpots. (Robert D. Higginbotham, APO, N.Y.)

Fish Eyes and Glue. Tapioca. A kid's word from a woman who still can't look at tapioca without this image coming into her mind. (CFOS) Warren R. Johnston of Woolwich, Maine, who grew up in the '20s and '30s, said that he used this expression when he was growing up, as did his wife, Bobby, who grew up in the '30s and '40s.

This entry brings up the important matter of names that kids give to school cafeteria food. In September, 1976, the London *Observer* ran a contest to get "the most tasty and inventive alternative names for school food." Some that were published:

Socks on a radiator = cheese on toast.
Floating tonsils = plums in juice.
Brylcreem = white sauce.
Dead man's leg = jellyroll.
Compost heap = cole slaw.
North Sea oil = gravy.
Nun's boots = liver.
Drainpipe dip = macaroni soup.
Septic toes = stewed pears.
Peat bog = rhubarb pie.
Baby couldn't help it = trifle.

Stews could create a whole glossary of their own, but it would be hard to beat *Train Smash*, an old British military term for stews using a lot of tomato.

Fishflops. Those stringy things trailing behind the fish in an aquarium. "We live on a farm," writes Sally P. Knight of Westbrook, Maine, "therefore, if a cow drops cowflops, a fish must drop fishflops."

Flanhopper. The kind of spatula that you flip pancakes with, as opposed to a long, thin-bladed spatula for icing. A California man got his from his Georgia wife's family. (KNBR)

Flap. Word used in a family where the parents decided that the children should not say *fart*. One of those children is now middle-aged, and she still cannot keep a straight face when someone talks about the big flap at the PTA meeting. (KGO)

Flathead. Species of bird that flies into picture windows. (Allison Parker-Hedrick, Virginia Beach, Va.)

Fleckels. Black crust on the top of catsup bottles. (Robert Prokop, Sherwood Park, Alb.)

Flibble. To jiggle a loose button or tooth with one's finger. (Colin Howard)

Flim-flam-flooie. The large, interesting packages that fill the house just before Christmas. (Lynn Clark, Kirk, Col.)

Flimp. Feeling one gets from being up all night with a child or children. It is a different feeling from, say, staying up all night figuring out one's taxes. (KMOX)

Flinkus. Object that defies identification. That which was left in the garage by the last owner when you bought the house. (KNBR)

Floodle. An item—an ashtray, book, pencil, whatever—that when held gives that person the floor. This occasions the cry of "Who has the floodle?"

when more than two people are talking at the same time. From Jeanne Schrieber of Kailua-Kona, Hawaii, who developed the term with her three sisters.

Flopsweat. One actor's term for a particular aura that occurs during a failing play. (WNYC)

Flummle. To come up with a plausible explanation or answer when you really have no idea what you are talking about. From Nancy Craig of New Hope, Pennsylvania, who thinks it might have come from an old-time radio show, for example, "The Great Gildersleeve" or "Duffy's Tavern."

Flustrated. Combination of *flustered* and *frustrated*. Several people reported it, including writer Arnold R. Isaacs, who says, "I heard it from the cook, an archetypical Yankee grandmother, in a failing roadhouse in rural New Hampshire where I worked briefly as a waiter in 1958 or 1959. Whether it was a regionalism or her own invention I have no idea, but I've always thought it a marvelous word that deserves to be in the language. I presume it could also have a noun form, *flustration*."

Foiling. Peeling, after a sunburn. (WIND)

Fonching. Playful fighting among dogs. Ozarkian. (KMOX)

Fonj. (Pl. *Fonjes*) "These are little particles which spew out of an open light socket," writes John G. Hedemann of Kailua-Kona, Hawaii. "You could pull your shirt up and over your nose so that you wouldn't inhale them, but they still could stick to your body and make you sick if you didn't put a bulb in the socket right away and frantically brush the things off."

Foosty. Feel of an unused room. (KMOX)

Footsies. Pieces found at the bottom of a box of animal crackers, composed mostly of animal feet. (Carol Andresen)

Forgetabilia. The opposite of memorabilia, coined by Clifton Fadiman.

Foricksabundy. Condition of very high energy in a child; "Nancy is getting a bit foricksabundy. Maybe she should be encouraged to play outside." (WIND)

Formal Dances. Male sex organs in one family. It started with a great aunt years ago. The female equivalents are known as *mumu*, a term that was introduced to the family by an R.N. There are many examples of these in families, as well as examples of pet names for privates. In a column in *The Listener*, British writer Fritz Spiegl says that his daughters used "front-bum" and "back-bum" to distinguish between the lower private areas.

In her paper entitled "Genital Pet Names: Regularities in 'Personal' Naming Behavior" (presented at the 1982 meeting of the American Anthropological Association), Martha Carnog discusses dozens of examples—usually used in private between consenting adults. Carnog found among other things that Virginia was the most popular female genital name, stemming in part from the "Virginia is for lovers" slogan.

Fowlenzia. One of many names for the unspecified disease that attacks children when they either (a) don't wash their hands, (b) eat too much Halloween candy, or (c) let the dog lick their faces. (Ed Spingarn) Other diseases of the same severity reported from various quarters include *scagamoga, peedilitus, lompocaro, scobosis, sloberdebosky, the dread mohogus, the punies, hilars of the kishkus, conkus boncus of the zorch, high-glockin' flips, the dreaded lerggy,* and *fisterous.*

Clearly, many families have found a need for such medical terminology, and some have become quite sophisticated in finding names for ailments. A letter from Robert Falk of Atlanta explains one such system: "When I was in high school a fellow student in biology class meant to say 'acromegaly' (a growth disorder) but instead said 'aquamiglio.' Now at our house any unexplained ache, illness, pain, or rash is diagnosed as aquamiglio. If possible, the prefex 'aqua-' is replaced by the part of the body in question. Thus a sore elbow is due to 'elbomiglio' and an earache is caused by 'earquamiglio.'"

Frabble. Audible flatulence. (KNBR)

Fraintance. State midway between an acquaintance, whom you may have only met once or twice, and a true friend, whom you feel close to and would do anything for. Created by a family that saw a clear need for such a word in English. (KNBR)

Framusracket. Noise made by searching through a box of small items; a scrounging noise. (Stephen Haase)

Franchesca. "A trashy, historical romance novel, as in 'I don't want to read *War and Peace*, I just want a Franchesca,'" says V. Elrod of Eureka, California. "This comes from the usual name for the heroine, as in 'Franchesca, her bosom heaving, clung to the handsome, young Captain Chauncey."

Frankenstart. Blend of Frankenstein + start. Reported and defined by Renee Charles of Green Bay, Wisconsin: "To begin a job you know you don't have time to do right (thus wasting time, energy and sometimes money on a worthless project) but yet you do it anyway."

Froggies. Footed pajamas. (K.L.F. Findell, Albuquerque, N.M.)

Frones. Particles that stick to plates. Applied in the sentence, "The dishes are clean except for a few frones." (WCKY)

Frou-frou. The ragged pieces hanging from a page that has been pulled from a spiral-bound notebook. From a man who had a college professor who warned students not to hand in assignments with frou-frou hanging from them. (KMOX.)

Frudenda. (Sing. *frudendum*) Items handmade by grandmothers and other elderly ladies using dry cleaner bags, nylon net, artificial flowers, and so forth. Purpose unknown. From Mary Ann Raimond, Boynton Beach, Florida, who says it was originally coined by her mother.

Frup. A contraction for "throw up," used when you are too sick to utter both syllables. (Diana Montague, Urbana, Ill.)

Fuccimanooli. Any very expensive, imported car. It came from a *Time* magazine commercial in which the very expensive but imaginary car was featured. (John A. Main)

Fungies. (Also, *Phungies*) Defined by Vicki Schooler of Boulder, Colorado, as "Small, light, white, irregularly shaped, cushiony pieces of foam used as packaging material. No other known uses except as filler for empty spaces in lieu of air, land-fill material, and in packaging/protecting other 'fungies' during shipment."

(Schooler's note defining this term, packed in a box of fungies, contained fungy facts as well, such as the fact that they come in three basic shapes: a fat S, a cap, and a thick figure 8.) See also *Ghost Poo* and *Yamulkettes.*

Futzamutza. This is what unlabeled cheeses that remain in the refrigerator too long become in one family. (WHDH)

53

F.U. & R.T.B. Full Up and Ready To Burst. Said when refusing a second or third helping.

Fuzzies. "Movements seen at the corners of one's eyes that stop when looked at directly," reports Nelson Hanke of Garfield, Arkansas, who adds, "This was related to me by the Danley family, who believed they were of a ghostlike nature, and observed that some houses had more than others."

— GAPOSIS —

Gafurdlapoop. Boy or girl who cries wolf; hence, a quick and convenient way of saying that a false alarm is being sounded. (Stephen Wells, New Canaan, Conn.)

Gapers. Women, usually elderly, who sit with their legs apart in public. (Gayle Grove, Hagerstown, Md.)

Gaposis. Condition describing a blouse one size too small, that puckers when buttoned. (Lillian Tudiver and others.)

Garch. Taste gland pain from excessive sourness, such as that from a pickle. (WCKY)

Garpe. Some eighty years ago a Maryland woman's mother's sister spelled a label for a jelly jar wrong; ever since *garpe* is what the family calls grape jelly.

Gasnoids. Word used to interrogate suspects when a toilet has not been flushed, "Did you leave gasnoids?" (Janet Jirouschek, Hackensack, N.J.)

Gazelle in the Garden. "I came from a Maine seafaring family when men were bewhiskered to protect them from the elements," writes Jane Tukey of

Bangor. "My grandfather and great aunt sailed from Millbridge, Maine, to the Orient and back with their mother and father for a number of years. . . . Growing up, family dinners were always memorable experiences with word games in progress—especially during the carving time. On one such occasion, my great-aunt said quietly to her husband,'Fletcher, gazelle in the garden.' Whereupon, he took his napkin and carefully wiped off his soiled whiskers. To this day, we use that expression at the table to inform a person that they have some extra food on their face."

Apparently the food-on-the-face problem is common enough to generate a number of family code words. A New Hampshire woman tells a similar story about the variant *The gazelle's on the lawn* and adds that *Johnson's at the door* was originally used by her grandmother to let her grandfather know that he had produced a droplet at the end of his nose. Poet and anthologist William Cole reports that his Aunt Jane used *There is a gazelle in the park,* and Susan Jordan Everton of Norfolk, Virginia, says that her family uses the name *Mr. Nicholson,* after a sloppy eater who used to board with her great-grandmother.

Gazoomba. (1) A dead animal that has been run over so many times that it is impossible to tell what kind of creature it was. (2) By extension, any undesirable particle or additive in food, for example, "Any gazoombas in that hamburger?" (Dan McKenney, San Diego, Cal.)

Gazunda. Toilet pot that "gazunda" the bed. This is an old one reported from several families that may well have broken out of the realm of just a few families. (CFOS, WIND, etc.) Not to be confused with *gozinta,* which is a mathematical term in some families: "Three *gozinta* nine three times."

Geese. A password for many, many years, it is used by the kids to recognize or identify a family member. "He's got to be invited, he's geese."

Geshnells. Dense clutter. (WCKY)

Ghost Poo. White, styrofoam packing pieces. This is from Sally L. Brune of Ocean Springs, Mississippi, who says the term originally came from an Erma Bombeck column, but has become part of the vocabulary of her household.

Gifts. White specks on fingernails. This was given as a family word by a woman calling a radio call-in show in San Francisco. It is interesting because the word with the very same meaning appears in the recently republished *Hallamshire Glossary,* put together by the Rev. Joseph Hunter more than 150 years ago to record the localisms in use in Sheffield, England, between 1790 and 1810.

Gilagahoos. Small spots of light that are reflected off glass or water and dance around the room. (CFQC)

Glick. Name given to any type of casserole dish that requires pasta, soup, and any other soft ingredients. From Judy Pemberton of St. Louis, Missouri, who adds that the word comes from the "glick sound" that such food makes when it is spooned onto a plate, or when a large glob is shaken off the end of the spoon.

Glippy. Almost but not quite nauseous. From Sally Godfrey of Eastbrook, Maine, who explains, "We once had a very ladylike afghan hound who had a delicate stomach. She was a great one for dramatically lifting her head, sort of burping, then swallowing (which, if you try it, makes a 'glip' noise in the back of your throat when you start to swallow).

Hence a 'glippy stomach' is one just short of being nauseous."

Globies. The exposed portion of buttocks which show beneath short shorts and and some bathing suits. (Joanne Evans, Fort Myers, Fla.)

Gluebottom. A visitor who won't go away. Term contained in a letter from Logan Pearsall Smith to Edward Marsh of October 12, 1944. It appears in *A Chime of Words*, the recent collection of Smith letters edited by the late Edwin Tribble. Smith was a great lover and collector of "words privately invented by some groups and families," and in 1945, shortly before his death, he proposed publishing them but never did. A few from the collection appear, along with *gluebottom*, in the Marsh letter. See also *Milver* and *Onways,* which also come from the letter.

G.M.P.O.T. A Chicago woman told me that G.M.P.O.T. was her children's answer to F.H.B. It is pronounced *gimpot* and stands for Guests Making Pigs Of Themselves. A Washington, D.C., man says that *gimpot* had become common enough by the time his kids were growing up so that it had become camouflaged as *jampots.* J. Russell Edgerton of Taunton, Massachusetts, says that in his family G.M.P.O.T. was prefaced by F.P.I. for "Family Pitch In . . ."

Goat. Food that is put away or refrigerated for preservation, from a Marlin Perkins "Wild Kingdom" episode in which a live goat is staked out as lure for carniverous Komodo dragons. In the winter this family often puts food cooked ahead in a VW camper to cool so as not to waste refrigerator electricity, which occasions the question, "Have you put the goat in the car?" (Janet W. Crampton)

Godinga. Thing that cannot be fixed, such as the handle of a coffee cup. (WRC)

Goija. Blanket fuzz. "How did she get so much *goija* on her lollipop?" *aka Gikkies.*

Gollyrumps. State of nervousness associated with a happy event—"He gets the gollyrumps every Christmas morning." (WCKY)

Gollywobble. One of many names for the infant's pacifier. Others collected: *zoogie, binky, meadie, uh-oh, nippy, bubou, choopy, plug, noochie, nooch, loonge,* and *mi-nee.*

Gom or Gomdegom. Good fun, exciting. Used synonymously with *good,* but with more feeling. (Stephen V. Masse, Amherst, Mass.)

G.O.M.B. Acronym for Get Off My Back, used in anti-nagging campaigns. Reported by a number of people.

Gonger. A gift that is *too* practical (such as an ironing board, car jack, or coat hangers). From Nancy Skewis of Yelm, Washington, who explains its history: "It originated from my sister-in-law's family and mine is now using it. They had an Aunt Gonger whose husband *always* gave her one of these gifts for all occasions (including Valentine's Day!)."

Gonk. That which sticks to you—burrs, labels, tape, etc. (WIOD)

Goobies. Collective term for all the things that a teenager should not do. It is used in one family as shorthand before the kids go out in the evening: "Beware of the goobies." (WIND)

Goobiness. That bothersome feeling that you have forgotten to do something that you *know* you really did do, such as when you close your front door, walk away, and then keep wondering if you locked the door, even though you are almost positive that you did. (Steve Fergenbaum, Glen Rock, N.J.)

Gooboo. That which oozes and requires attention,

whether it be from the nose of a child or the engine of a car. (Myra Patner)

Googol. That rarest of words, one that leapt from the mouth of a child right into all the major dictionaries. When American mathematician Edward Kasner asked his nine-year-old nephew to come up with a word for 1 followed by 100 zeroes, the boy shot back with *googol*.

Googumpucky. A longer word should not be used when a smaller one will do, but this word for glue from the Nesbit family of Eugene, Oregon, is an exception.

Gookimo. Short for "Look, the baby is doing something cute. Don't do anything to distract him/her." Patricia Goff of Calais, Maine, says of the term, "The word is always said in an undertone to adults only, accompanied by a nod of the chin in the direction of the child." She adds that it may be of Pennsylvania Dutch origin.

Gooper Feathers. "The fuzz from peaches," according to an Amos 'n' Andy phonograph record from the late 1920s or thereabouts. Adopted by some younger members of that generation (1) as a euphemism for obscenity they did not yet dare use, or (2) to signify something useless or uninteresting. (Warren Johnston)

Gopie. Something used by supermarkets to operate automatic doors. Invented by the sister of Donna Turner, who reports, "To this day, we still say 'thanks, gopie' when passing through."

Gourmet Parent. Those who would have toddlers studying Russian, claim their children would rather be at the National Gallery of Art than Disneyworld, and would opt for a good nutritious lentil soup over a Whopper and Fries. The term was heard on a radio discussion of "parenting."

These parents talk differently. At a "Children's Festival" at Wolf Trap Farm in Virginia, I heard a G.P. tell a misbehaving child of about five: "Joshua, I am running out of caring energy." A non-G.P. would say, "Joshua, if you don't knock it off, we're going home." Or, a G.P. father watching a youngster spitefully destroy a silk flower in a department store, "Jason, say goodbye to Mr. Flower."

The ultimate GP question came on a Washington radio call-in show on which the the guest was a childhood development expert.

GP: I'm worried that my daughter's linguistic development is being neglected. Could you suggest a good set of phonic flash cards?

Expert: How old is she?

GP: Three months.

Grabacabbage. Generic name for a person whose name is difficult to pronounce. Usually understood in context, such as "the little Grabacabbage kid," or "the Grabacabbage dog." (Russ Dunn, Sr.)

Grackles. Raisinlike wrinkles on fingertips from spending a long time in the water. Upon hearing this reported on a San Francisco talk show, another person called in to say that these were *shivels* in his family. (KGO)

Gradoo. Miscellaneous dirt, junk, small pieces of grit, etc. The sludge at the bottom of wash water, or what's left after melting snow for drinking water, is *gradoo.* Several reports of this word indicate a fairly broad circulation. Sometimes spelled *gradu.*

Grandma's Beads. The combination of sweat, dust and dirt that kids get in the creases of their necks; little beads of mud. (Patsy Jett, Hillsboro, Mo.)

Green Caboose. Anything that defies belief. Dates from the decision by the old Penn Central Railroad to paint all of its cars lime green, including the caboose, which, as everyone knows, should be red. (Carole A. Digel, Forest Hill, Md.)

Greenebaum. In Irv Kupcinet's *Kup's World,* the story is told that the Greenebaum banking firm held the mortgage on the Marx Brothers' family home. The boys' mother always worried about making the payments; so she would stand in the wings while the boys performed and would yell "Greenebaum!" whenever one of them strayed from the script.

Gretchen. A fabrication created about one's self; a bogus piece of personal history. Reported by Stacy Tatman of Lake Mary, Florida, who says it all started years ago when a friend told a story about how she was forced to wear her hair in braids pinned to her head. This, she said, caused all her classmates to call her Gretchen. Later "Gretchen" admitted that the whole thing was made up.

Grezeti. An unnamed or unknown volume or quantity, such as "There is a *grezeti* of ice cream left in the freezer." (Cate Pfeifer, Milwaukee, Wis.)

Grice. The frozen substance that accumulates in large blocks behind the back wheels of cars in winter. It is a combination of dirt, snow, and ice. The word *grice* combines the words *grime* and *ice*. This is referred to as *snard* in another family, as *snowlactites* in another, and as *carsicle* in still another. Clearly the English language really lets us down here, as so many people have had to create their own word for this. *Grice* is a good, logical candidate, as is *snirt* or, for that matter, *slud, knobacles*, and *snowtice*.

Griefcase. Child's name for the briefcase in which his father, a professor, brought home his bluebooks for grading. The boy is now a lawyer and has a griefcase of his own. (Ruth Bauerle, Delaware, Oh.)

Gripsion. Child's blend of *grip* and *traction*. (WIND) Also reported by a New Hampshire family where it is spelled *gription* and is almost always used when suction or adherence is lacking. (P.F. Smith, Hollis, N.H.)

Gritch. Blend of *gripe* + *bitch*. (KNBR)

Grose Baboune. An unhappy child with lower lip extended in the traditional pout. French origin. (Tammy Chadbourne, Southington, Conn.)

Grundle. A small infant's mode of locomotion before learning to crawl properly. (C. Dick, Corvallis, Ore.)

Guano. Benjamin Disraeli campaigned to have this noun (for sea-bird manure) turned into a verb. Lady Constance in his novel *Tancred, or The New Crusade*, "... guanoed her mind by reading French novels."

Gulge. To move unnecessarily; to fidget. (Johnathan Tourtellot, Washington, D.C.)

Gumbacco. The July 4, 1977, issue of *Sports Illustrated* says that this is a mixture favored by a small circle of baseball players.

Gummidgey. Fretful, self-pitying, and forlorn. "I was really feeling gummidgey last night." Word that one couple derived from the character of Mrs. Gumidge in Charles Dickens's *David Cooperfield*, who utters lines like, "Nothinks nat'rel to me but to be lone and lorn." (KNBR)

This would not be the first name from Dickens to become a word. In *Thou Improper, Thou Uncommon Noun*, Willard R. Espy points to these, among others: from Mr. Pickwick came *pickwickian* for something not to be taken seriously; from Mr. Micawber came *micawberish* for being doggedly optimistic despite constant adversity; from Mr. Pecksniff we got *pecksniffian* for hypocrisy or unctuous insincerity, and from Mr. Podsnap we got *podsnappery* for self-satisfied philistinism. Espy adds that other characters have become general names for their characteristics, including *Fagin* for a thief-trainer, *Scrooge* for a cantankerous miser, and *Uriah Heep* for a sanctimonious hypocrite.

Gummatajuma. To ride over the railroad tracks in the car, from the noise made.(KGO)

Gungales. [gungaliyz.] Rice, ravioli, noodles, and other starchy foods collectively, especially when cut up. (Herbert Paper, Cincinnati, Oh.)

Gurker. Rubber sink stopper, renamed for the "gurk gurk" noise it makes when pulled. (Anna Lee)

Gwee. The by-product of frequent erasing and, by extension, any small and crumbly mess, such as the fragments found in the bottoms of toasters. (Mary Eccher, Oak Park, Ill.)

Gwell or Guell. Undercooked egg white. (Stephen V. Masse) Another contributor called it *quebble*, which is a separate entry because its definition is broader.

— A HANDSOME MAN —

Hahas. Child's word for glasses. The term comes from the sound you make when you breathe heavily on them to steam them up for cleaning. Hahas, which is spelled "h-a-h-a-s," should actually be pronounced with a loud breathy sound. (WPLP)

Halacious. In the extreme; usually applied positively (a halacious bikini) but not without its negative use (I was fighting this halacious headache).

This is one of those words that people regard as their own; but which trips off many tongues. In his last book, *Good Words to You*, John Ciardi discusses the word as "fad slang" and suggests its roots are in the Yiddish *chalusus,* for terrible or disastrous. Ciardi made the point that the sense reversal from the tragic to the halacious (of the halacious hot fudge sundae) follows the pattern established, for example, in the black English use of bad for good.

Handibles. Those things that are too big to go into the dishwasher and must be done by hand. Handibles are often a male province. (KNBR)

A Handsome Man. Reply to the criticism that one is

dressed sloppily. It is short for a line from Walt Kelly's *Pogo* comic strip, "A handsome man looks good in anything he throws on." (Jane and Paul Hinckley, Hicksville, N.Y.)

Hannah Cook. The expression "not worth Hannah Cook" had been used by a Maine mother to express worthlessness. Many years later her son, George Whitin, learned that it came from an old seafaring expression "not worth a hand or a cook"—that is, not worth the lowest ranking members of a ship's crew.

Happyluia. Word coined for Easter hymns by a young daughter in a New York family. Makes sense. (Timothy B. Messick)

Haranagged. Improved version of *harangued,* created by poet and novelist Stephen Vincent Benét as a child and later reported by his brother poet and critic, William Rose Benét.

Harthing. Hot and panting, as in a harthing dog. (Mike Hartnett, Willoughby, Oh.)

Haschoo. As defined by Counsel Langley, age twelve, Port Townsend, Washington, "The period of time between fluffing up the pillows, turning off the reading lamp, and actually falling off to sleep. The word comes from the little sighs of comfort made as you snuggle down under the covers and relax."

Haysa-donde. A fine term that requires a background before definition. It comes from David Andrew Saltzman of Chatham, New Jersey, who tells the story:

"My grandfather founded a synagogue in Paterson, N. J., around World War I. Although a reverent place, it was a congregation of hard-working men who had an admirable sense of humor and proportion.

"To 'assist' the Rabbi in keeping order, someone would stand up at his seat and shout, 'Hey, sit down there!' to anyone talking. In his broken English, it would sound more like 'Haysa-donde.' The wise guys didn't like being told this and called the helper a haysa-donde for butting in.

"This has been passed along to my father and to me. To this day, when we hear someone acting like a bigshot at a gathering we'll look at each other and one of us will say ... 'haysa-donde.' I can't think of any other expression which so perfectly describes this type of individual."

Hective. *Hectic + active.* (WHJJ)

Herbies. Any offensive insects, especially roaches. Created as a play on the word "herbivore" and used in an attempt to alert family members to their presence without dismaying guests (e.g., Could you please come here, dear, Herbie just arrived). (Tamarah Malley, of Fort Belvoir, N.J.)

Higgens. Name for hens and chickens together; birds that live in "higgen houses." (Sally P. Knight)

Higollics. An encompassing word for any form of mild gastric distress from heartburn to indigestion. From Joyce Reynolds Kurth, whose father, Walt Reynolds, has suffered the higollics for many years.

Hippocanereous. Noisy; out of control; kids on a rainy day.(WIND)

Hobbiehie. [hobbie-hi] Person whose gender is not apparent at first glance. Invented by kids who, on long automobile trips, would bet on whether they would pass more men or women. One kid would keep score while the other would yell "man," "woman," or, when in doubt, "hobbiehie." (WRC)

Hoddibithchew. That which is left in the tub after you have bathed and drained the water. (Sharon A. Harris, Lewiston, Me.)

HOLLAND. Versatile acronym that variously stands for Hope Our Love Lasts And Never Dies and Have On Little Lace And No Drawers. This is one of many such acronyms and initialisms of which the most famous is SWAK (for Sealed With A Kiss). Others like RPRLH for "Run Postman, Run Like Hell" have fallen into disuse and mainly appear in packets of old love letters.

Homestead. (V.) To stop your car and wait in a likely place for a parking space, as in "You get out and I'll homestead for a while." (Judith Sarah Cohen, Los Angeles, Cal.)

Hometel. Tourist home; bed and breakfast. (Anne Higgins, from her young son)

Hoojackapivvy. A family term for any object such as a whatchamacallit, whose name did not come readily to mind. (John Duffie, Victoria, B.C.) There are many other such names including the imposing *Klappestranger.*

Hoop. The act of bending down over a glass of milk or other beverage that is filled to the brim and slurping up enough liquid so that the glass may be picked up without spilling. From Jan Holloway of St. Louis who says the word came from "the sound made when performing this necessary action."

Hoora's Nest. (alt. Hurra's Nest, Hooraw's Nest, Hurrah's Nest, etc.) An untidy mess; a jumble of unrelated items. Reported by Donald W. Athearn of Concord, New Hampshire, and several other New Englanders. It appears to be an old regional expression that lives on in some families.

Charles Earle Funk discussed this odd and rare term in his book *Heavens to Betsy! And Other Curious Sayings.* He traced it back to 1829 and its appearance as a "family term" in Samuel Longfellow's biography of his brother Henry Wadsworth Longfellow. Funk also found the term in Richard Henry Dana's 1840 work *Twenty Years Before the Mast* and notes that Dana studied under Henry Wadsworth Longfellow at Harvard.

Horserubbish. Horseradish in the family of Frank Muir, who reported it on the BBC's "My Word."

Hoybee. The swirled pattern of hair that can be seen on the head of a short-haired boy. This and the next item came from the Roussos family of Concord, New Hampshire.

Hozey. A dibs word, as in "I hozey the wayback." Especially interesting in that it gave birth to *hozey-not,* meaning "I won't do it," or "I don't want it." See also *Huh* for more dibs words.

Huey. The feeling in the pit of the stomach when the family car hits a sharp dip in the road. (Gary MacShara, Harrodsburg, Ky.) Sally White, who grew up in western Pennsylvania, says that in her family the response to such a dip was "Oh, I got ink in my stomach." Several families insist that this is a *whoop-de-doo.* See also *Thank-you-ma'am.*

Huffle and Kefuffle. A term used by a British family to describe an atmosphere of confusion, cross-purposes, and general uproar. (It was reported by Warren and Bobby Johnston, who learned it from a delightful English lady they met on a bus tour in Greece. "She used it to characterize the tremendous uproar and confusion attending the loading of cars and passengers onto a Greek ferry—a quite normal circumstance for which the Greek word is *fasaria.*")

Huggle. *Hug + Snuggle.* It is a word that has been discovered in many families.

Huh. To claim as one's own, from an act in which a kid breathes heavily (huuuuh!) on something to establish ownership. "I huh the icing in the bowl." The woman who reported it on a Cincinnati radio show initially defined it as "to *thinny* something." It was quickly determined that "thinny" was an old neighborhood term for claiming possession. (WCKY) *Coz on* was another that showed up.

Terms of possession, like *huh* and *thinny*, have long been common among kids. In their 1959 classic, *The Lore and Language of Schoolchildren*, Iona and Peter Opie note that the most common British term for possession is *bags* in various forms ("bags it to me," "baggy mine," etc.), but they also found a number of other regional and neighborhood words for the same act. The Opies collected *ballow, barley, bollars, chaps, chucks, chops, cogs, ferry, fogs, jigs it, nab it, nag it, pike I, sags, shigs,* and *whack it.*

Humbly. Not the adverb, but an adjective that is a cross between *humble* and *homely.*

A significant family word in that it is used as the prime example in one of the first articles ever on the family word. An unsigned article in the November 1908 issue of *Atlantic* on "Improvised Words" introduces it: "There is hardly a family but has some expressive improvised word. In my own family 'humbly' reigns supreme . . . it was first used to describe our washwoman, who takes such pride in her humbleness, and is of such a superlative weatherbeaten homeliness, that she needed something special to express her personality." See also *neb, pang-wangle, streely,* and *tod,* which are from the same article.

Hunna. That wet spot on the pillow case you discover upon waking that proves you've been drooling in your sleep. (Tobey Levine, Sharon, Vt.)

Hyorky. The generic name for a far-off place. From a Rhode Island woman whose family acquired it many years ago. Interesting case, because it is listed in William F. Macy's *Nantucket Scrap Basket* as a word peculiar to the island. Macy defines it as "Some far-off outlandish place: 'He's gone to Hyorky.'"

— I-I's —

Iguanas. The little brown, burnt potato chips that come in every bag, which you inadvertently eat. (Nancy Mayerman, Williamsville, N.Y.)

I-I's. Short for MacDonald's, probably deriving from "Old MacDonald Had a Farm" and the lyric "ee-ii-ee-ii-oh." (Jean Stockton, Mableton, Ga.)

Implatenate. An object on a desk that gets in the way of one's typewriter carriage. When on the left, the implatenate causes the letters to pile up before the end of the line. Right-hand implatenates inhibit the carriage return, so a line is suddenly irregularly indented. (Patricia Spaeth, Seattle, Wash.)

Insinuendo. At once a blend of and a synonym for *insinuation* and *innuendo*.

This word has been offered as a family word by at least three people, but it has a long history, being "coined" regularly ever since it first showed up in Samuel Butler's *The Way of All Flesh*, in which a character says, "I hate his nasty insinuendos." An article entitled "Biography of the Word 'Insinuendo'" appears in the February 1932 issue of

American Speech and outlines many of the incidents in which people have claimed its coinage. The article also mentions the "nearly synonymous" *hintimation.*

Intertwingled. A blend of *intertwined* and *intermingled.* Reported by Jean E. Smythe of Calgary, Alberta, who says it was coined by her daughter Hilary when she was eight or ten. "It was first used and is generally still used (ten years later) in a game of gin rummy when your sets and runs are so mixed up you can't sort them out and don't know what to throw away [but it] has plenty of other applications."

It was delicious. Ritualistic response to any question beginning with the words, "Have you seen my ___ ?" (Sally C. Knight)

It was Milk Duds. Anything that proves to be easier or less frightening than originally feared to be. Applied to final exams, driving tests, visits to the dentist, and so on. This family phrase was reported by Barb Hanselman of Angola, Indiana, who tells how it started.

"Not yet two years old, my 'baby sister' got into my middle sister's top dresser drawer (the dresser was alongside her crib) and found a package of Milk Duds, opened the package and ate the chocolate off a couple. Then she fell asleep (she'd been put down for her afternoon nap). When my mother went to check on her, she was standing up in the crib, holding onto the rail, grinning widely and covered all over with brown splotches. She'd fallen asleep on the scattered Milk Duds and the chocolate had melted. However, mother feared the worst and she made *me* go in and check my sister. I discovered the empty box and several caramel centers among the sheets and began laughing. As Mom ran in, I said, "It's OK, Mom, it's only Milk Duds.""

— JIGGER —

Japocky. This is, in one family, the word for the particular type of behavior that kids engage in to delay going to bed. Checking to make sure that your milk money is in your book bag after the Cosby Show is over is the most blatant japocky. (WAMU)

Jet Leg. A foot that has fallen asleep on a long flight; that which happens to a kid's leg on an airplane. From an unidentified ten-year-old quoted in the July 1984 *Reader's Digest*.

Jigger. The circle of bone in a large slice of ham. "My brother and I would always argue over who was to have the 'jigger,' although I'm not sure what we did with it once we got it," says Patricia Goff of Calais, Maine, who reported this important term.

Juvember. An unspecified, far-off date, usually stated as "next Juvember." Juvember is to months what umpteen and umpty-ump are to numbers. (Michele Newton Dohse, Asheville, N.C.)

— KAHLITZ —

K. A joke, usually an in-house one, whose meaning is only known to the family. It is pronounced "kay" and is commonly used when another family member doesn't get a joke and has to be reminded of its intramural meaning. (Jean Scott Creighton)

(It is interesting to note that the character Willie Clark in Neil Simon's *The Sunshine Boys* announces "Words with a *k* in them are funny. If it doesn't have a *k* in it, it's not funny." Clark explains that "chicken and pickle" are funny but that "tomato and roast beef" are not.)

Kahlitz. The white lines on the top of a cup of tea when the water wasn't quite boiled all the way— taken from the German word for undercooked, raw spots in cake. From Sher Bird Garfield, who says her father hated such tea and used to confound waiters and waitresses by telling them, "Take this back; it has kahlitz."

Karate Ants. Martin S. Kottmeyer reports, "There are several ways you can tickle a person, and one of the most maddening ways to do it is to take out your two index fingers and rapidly, randomly attack the victim's abdomen. My nephew came at me with this torture technique a couple of years ago and when he does it he adds a battle cry . . . 'karate ants, karate ants, karate ants.' Naturally anytime we threaten each other with this torture we refer to it as karate ants."

K.B. Kidney Buster. Used by more than one family to order a very watered down drink, say, one ounce of liquor to ten of water or soda. Employed when the liquor stock was low or when the person just wanted a weak drink. "Mix me a K.B., I'm driving." (WRC)

Kerfunkle. Cry that goes up when a car is spotted with one back light out. *Pididdle, unikey,* and *popeye* are all common terms for burnt-out headlights. These cries are used to keep score as kids try to spot missing lights for points. (KGO, WXYZ, WRC, etc.) *Fladiddlem* is a rare term for the same thing offered by Tracy Cobbs, as is *Diddlap* from Rick Zimmerman of South Euclid, Ohio. *Unibee,* on the other hand, is a motorcycle that is often mistaken for a pididdle according to Debra Elkins of Amherst, Virginia.

Khulyages. (rhymes with "fool wages") A fascinating coinage of Dr. Gerald Phillips, who teaches speech at Pennsylvania State University. Back in 1969 Phillips and about 200 of his students got the idea that they would see if they could get the word in the dictionary. Dubbed "The Great Khulyages Conspiracy," the word came from Phillips's love of doubletalk and his discovery that no word of English origin began with the letters KH. (Words that show up in collegiate dictionaries, like khaki, khan, and khedive, are all taken directly from other languages.)

After getting other university speech departments to join the conspiracy, Phillips was quoted, "If we start khulyages simultaneously in Pennsylvania and Montana, by the time it reaches Illinois, it may mean something."

It never did make the dictionary, but in the months that followed, it had a glorious life. A bakery in California created a khulyages donut, the University of Tennessee football team had a khulyages play, a business consultant launched the "Greater Atlanta Khulyages Campaign" to attract industry, and a woman bridge expert began using it to describe the worst hand one was dealt in that game. In all, Phillips got some 400 letters, most of which attempted to give it a meaning. Only one, however, seemed to fit. It appeared in an anonymous note slipped under Phillips's door, which read, "Khulyages is a situation in which alternatives are perfectly clear, but what is not clear is whether the alternatives are any better than the situation. Example: You're in a cafeteria and you have a tuna and noodle casserole in front of you when all of a sudden you realize they're also serving sloppy Joes and chop suey."

Kidults. Adults or kids that are supposed to be adults. (Janet Pugh, Edwardsville, Ill.)

Kill-me-quick. Generic term for anything you want but which is probably not good for you—candy, chocolate eclairs, Cuban cigars, and the like. (Jay Ames, Toronto, Ont.)

Kinsprit. A contraction of "kindred spirit," created and advanced by author Christopher Morley, who wrote that it "seemed to me to fill the need for a term to express the relation among people who are enthusiastic about the same thing."

Kleenices. Plural form for the name of a popular facial

tissue, derived from the plural forms of index and appendix. (Robert P. Hesse, Falls Church, Va.)

Korvette. To drive about endlessly in a parking lot looking for a space. "I korvetted for about twenty minutes and then had to give up." From the place, a store in the now-defunct E. J. Korvette chain, where the family first did it. (Margaret Schweitzer)

Krunk. A person who cannot be pleased—"un-appeasable." "I tried to deal with him, but suddenly realized he was a krunk." (Janet W. Hook, Ridgefield, Conn.)

— LAPKIN —

Lapkin. A cloth napkin. The word, of course, contains a reminder of where it belongs. (Renee Epstein, Great Neck, N.Y.), Another family using the word says *kneepkin* for a lapkin that has slipped out of place. (Sandra M. S. Kent, Akron, Oh.)

Larp. To be blinded by light, as when the lights are turned on in a dark room or a flash bulb is exploded unexpectedly. Created by two English teachers attempting to get a word to fit a common situation. "I was almost asleep when she larped me." (KNBR)

Larrupin Truck. Good food, from a Texas woman. (KNBR)

Laundry Ball. A boring basketball game; a game with the same monotonous quality as laundry going around and around in a washing machine. (Karen Feinberg, Cincinnati, Oh.)

Lazy Jim. A man who grew up in Florida said that this is what all the kids in his neighborhood called the heat ripples that come up from paved roads on very hot, sunny days. (WRC)

L, E and W. Short for Leave Early and Walk. Used for

a person who wants to go when the driver and the rest of the family do not. It is stated as if the L, E and W were a train. (Tamara L. Harless, Huntington, West Va.)

Leaverite. Name for a rock or mineral that one Iowa man's father couldn't identify. It was, he discovered, short for "Leave her right there." (WHO) Apparently, leaverite is not an uncommon term among the "family" of rock hunters and geologists. There are variations as well. *Heaverite*, according to Raymond J. Nelson of Cody, Wyoming, is a rock that, upon examination, is only good to "heave 'er right now." Geologist David Dattie of Spring Valley, Minnesota, reports *Nebulite* is a rock you cannot identify—a rock of unknown or nebulous origin.

Lemon. The number after ten. (Fran Urban)

Le Petit Ondu. In French, the little place, and the term for bathroom in one family. A woman in the family says that she was in a department store in Paris and was in great need of such a place. Unable to think of the right term, she blurted out to a sales clerk, "Où est le petit ondu?" The clerk broke up because she said that was what it was called in her family.

Let's get out before we're blew out. Expression from the family of John Duffie, who wrote of it in one of his columns on family words and expressions in *Monday* magazine of Victoria, B.C. He explains, "In my younger days, my mother used to employ a young man for handyman jobs around the house. Johnnie was what we would call today a slow learner, but he was a willing and conscientious worker. One day the hot water tank in the kitchen began to clank and make ominous hissing noises. Mother looked to Johnnie, as the nearest grown-up male, to take charge, but all he said was 'Let's get out before we're blew out.' For years, every impending disaster in our home drew the comment . . ."

Linoleum. Word used whenever a family member does not want to do something or loan something but lacks a real, legitimate excuse to say "No." It is the response to a question like "Why can't I borrow your baseball glove?" It comes from Morton Goldberg of Binghamton, New York, who says the word came from an Andy Capp cartoon in which the following interchange took place:

> *Other person:* "Andy, can I borrow your can opener?"
>
> *Andy:* "No."
>
> *Other person:* "Why not?"
>
> *Andy:* "I need it to cut linoleum."
>
> *Other person:* "You can't cut linoleum with a can opener."
>
> *Andy:* "I can if I don't want to lend it to you."

Lint Galaxy. That which surfaces on the lint-removing screens of washing machines and dryers. Used to justify the "spinning cloud of dust and dirt" theory of creation. (Janet Mangalvedhe, Baltimore, Md.)

A Lion. This family word dates back to a living room slide show given by a rather dull friend on his return from Africa. A slide of a lion came on the screen, and he said, "A lion." Ever since, anything that is patently obvious is announced as "A lion." (WNYC)

The need to establish a noun for the patently obvious shows up in other families. After telling the story of "a lion" during a talk on family words given to the American Translators Association, I was handed a note by a man named Ben Teague, which

80

read: "*Ann Miller.* When my wife was a little girl, she interrupted a TV movie—all singing, all dancing—to ask her mother, 'Who's Ann Miller, Mummy?' [Her reply] 'A tap dancer.' Now it means 'A lion.'"

Living Room Quality. That which is only good enough to show to the relatives in the privacy of the family living room. In reality, it tends to refer to excruciatingly poor children's performances in the areas of music, dance, or acting. From Jane and Paul Hinckley, who first picked it up from a friend who owns a dancing school.

L.M.C. Low Marble Count. Used for anyone or anything that is not very bright. From Ann Zlamal of Phoenix, Arizona, who says there are several teachers in her family who created the term to discuss certain students in "non-professional" gatherings.

Lordies. Those unusually high waves at the seashore that unexpectedly dunk you completely, causing you to cough and splutter. From Julie Knippling of Villa Hills, Kentucky, who adds, "This word was coined in our family by my younger brother, who would let out an exuberant 'Lordy, Lordy' after being hit by one of these waves."

Lovely. A gift of undeterminable worth, tempting the recipient to write "Thank you for the lovely" in the thank-you note. Many wedding presents are lovelies. (Robert G. Chamberlain, San Marino, Cal.)

Lurkin. A single sock, so called because you know the mate is lurkin' around somewhere. (C.W. Sande, M.D., Caldwell, Ida.)

— MAD SCREAM LINES —

Mad Scream Lines. The levels dangerously near the top of the bath tub, inspired by the sound of the cry, "Turn the water off!" (Janet Mangalvedhe, Baltimore, Md.)

Make-tend. A delightful blend of make-believe and pretend. (Fay Donaghey, Pembroke, N.H.)

Maplejack. The name for the new (since 1965) Canadian flag in the family of Phillip Chaplin of Ottawa.

Masonite. In one Chicago family, anything that is not up to snuff, or that is a copy. (WIND)

Maude. Kitchen junk drawer; place for things that have no proper place. (Linda Schaub, Suffolk, Va.)

Maw Bread. Rye bread with caraway seeds. Etymology: "While attempting to remove the caraway seeds from his teeth with his tongue," says Norma Daniel of Escondido, California, "my father looked as though he was pronouncing the word 'maw.'"

McGuffin. Alfred Hitchcock's word for that which was sought after as the special element in each of his movies. It was recently used as the name of a Hitchcockian novel by John Bowen.

Meckensop. A waterproof coat in the family of Frank Muir of the BBC's "My Word."

Melvin. The rubbery crust that forms on the top of a pudding. A third generation family word believed to go back to a neighborhood kid named Melvin, who loved to scrape the "melvin" off a pudding. (WIND)

Meningus. To achieve a very difficult maneuver in sports, such as an "impossible" spare in bowling, a tough golf putt, or a tricky shot in billiards. From Tom Gill of Davis, California, who says it came from the surname of an individual who was locally legendary for such achievements. "His real name was something else, like Meniggus or Menegrus, but the term is definitely Meningus."

Menuitis. Having so many choices that you take forever to make up your mind. Shari Gackstatter of New Cumberland, Pennsylvania, says it was inspired by her sister who could never decide what to order in a restaurant. The rest of the family would explain to the waitress that she had menuitis.

Metutials. Small, irksome chores that must be done before anything else can be done. "I'll do it after my metutials" gives nasty tasks a certain dignity according to the woman whose family uses it. (WIOD)

M.F.A. Mandatory Family Attendance. Applied to certain events, usually initiated by parents. (Mrs. Thomas Polek, Los Gatos, Cal.)

Midas Words. Words that are so badly slurred that they are unclear or take on a new meaning. From Wilma P. Derting of Tucson, Arizona, who reports, "The phrase began when a young European girl, not yet proficient in slurred English, asked how to spell midas. Puzzled, my sister asked what she was trying to write. Her reply, 'Oh, you know, like, I midas well close the letter.'"

Miff. Sound emitted by a dog as it passes air from the mouth with just enough pressure to have jowls move and to allow a whiff of air to escape. (Donna Kipp, Rochester, N.Y.)

Milkdew. The dried milk at the bottom of a glass a few hours after someone drank the milk. (Andrea Veri)

Milkstache. Milk mustache in a number of families.

Milver. From the late essayist Logan Pearsall Smith, who defined it as a "name of someone who shares our admirations, ecstasies, and above all, our execrations." (Also a rhyme for the rhymeless word 'silver.')

Misewell. Associated tasks. "As long as we are painting the kitchen, we misewell paint the hall," or "The hall is a misewell." From M. A. Lange of Cleveland, Ohio, who collected it from a friend.

Mishok. Too much of something. A mishok dress has too many ruffles and mishok curtains too much design. (WIOD)

Mixmaster With Two B's. The creation of a youngster who considered it "a *real bad* word." Used for serious name-calling. (Mary J. Tanner, Weatherford, Tex.)

Mizzle. [mizz-el] To mislead in the extreme. From a family that believes there are times when the word *misled* sounds too tame and that mizzled is more to the point. (WIND)

(We learn in Alfred H. Holt's *Word and Phrase Origins* that mizzle was once a synonym for drizzle which has fallen by the wayside. This explains Thomas Hood's pun about George IV, in which he said the king first reigned then mizzled. John Ciardi references *mizle* in his *Second Browser's Dictionary* as a deliberate and unofficial pronunciation of mislead, as in, "He mizled and bed-raggled her.")

Moas. Round rolled hay bales as opposed to the rectangular boxy type. From Kathleen R. Hayes of Leavittsburg, Ohio, who reports, "This came about when my nephew indicated that they looked rather like the droppings of a very large animal, possibly from an extremely large moa (a moa is an extinct flightless bird from New Zealand which was sometimes twelve feet tall). Ever after those round hay bales were known to us as moa turds and finally just as moas, e.g., 'a field full of moas.'"

Modate. Defined by Karen Feinberg of Cincinnati, Ohio, "To talk a good game without accomplishing anything. To wait for your ship to come in when you haven't sent one out."

MODGOT. Short for "Money doesn't grow on trees." The antonym is *MINO* for "Money is no object." (Jerrold B. Schwartz, Atlanta, Ga.)

Mome. Someone not quite arrived at, but well on his way to the status of full blockhead. Not to be confused with the *sumph* who is the same person upon becoming a blockhead.

These words are not family words but could be since most families could use a few mild-sounding words of disapproval: "Don't be a mome, call her up and apologize."

Both these words appeared in a Norman Cousins editorial in the June 10, 1948, *Saturday Review* and were among those words which he decried were dying out. Forty years later they are totally dead and in need of revival. Cousins also argued for the preservation of *dumble*, the short form of dumbbell, and *chuff*, which he called "a Shakespearean favorite to describe someone who converts his extra wealth into extra chins."

Monsuvious. A state that is a notch above monstrous. Originally applied to ocean waves of great size. From a Rhode Island man who requested anonymity.

Mooching. Constant squirming motion, like a small child in a chair when she wants to get up, or in bed when she can't get to sleep. (Marjorie Linhares, Portsmouth, R.I.)

Moon Nuts. Cashews as renamed by a lad who could not say the proper name and noted that they resembled the quarter moon. (Marlene Heinen, Wright City, Mo.)

Morfusgorfus. That hair that grows on the back of the neck between haircuts. (KGO)

Morphendyke. Hermaphrodite. In a *Commonweal* essay entitled "When Words Go Private," John Garvey tells of hearing this word on a playground many years ago, and of how its impact was such that to this day "I always have to translate the word *hermaphrodite* into its *real* meaning before I can appreciate it." Garvey uses the word to lead up to this key point, "I don't know how much television has cut into children's culture, but that special world that exists on playgrounds and in vacant lots and alleys and places where children gather away from their elders is one of the last places where language still has its power as a form of magic. The magic was more common once."

Morrisism. A statement that is technically correct but nowhere near the truth. Named for a man who had mastered the art of telling a friend he did nothing all afternoon, but who neglected to point out that he had dated the friend's girlfriend that evening at 6:05. (KNBR)

Mothom. Something you keep but don't use. (WXYZ)

Mouse Pie. Dried beef. (Jane Tesh, Mount Airy, N.C.)

M.P. Initialism for Mother's Privilege, and a reply to questions like, "How come we have to eat all our vegetables and you don't?" From Susan Pinto of Yonkers, New York, who now invokes G.P. around her six grandchildren.

Mrs. Burgunda. From Patricia Jorgenson, who appears in *A Celebration of American Family Folklore*: "When we were kids and one of us wanted one thing and one of us wanted another, particularly in the way of food for dinner, my mother would say, 'I won't be a Mrs. Burgunda. I won't go crazy trying to satisfy all of you.' There was a story her mother had told about a woman who did just that, who tried to accommodate the tastes of each child separately. And one day she was just worn to a frazzle and she jumped out a window and committed suicide."

Mr. Smat. (Also Mrs./Miss/Ms. Smat) A person who is trying to impress everyone and just ends up making a fool out of him- or herself. "This comes from when my husband was in fifth grade," writes Anne Barnes of Wichita, Kansas, "and was going to show everyone how smart he was during parent-teacher conferences. Instead of putting his name on his desk, he wrote MR. SMART, only he misspelled it and instead it read MR. SMAT."

Muck-me-do-dah. Milk in one family. Reported by a woman who baby-sat for the family and who had to use the term as a requirement of employment. Today she recalls in horror, "Imagine being nineteen and being forced to say muck-me-do-dah."

Mudwaffles. Neatly shaped chunks of mud and dirt that are brought into the house on the soles of running shoes and boots. Claire Howard of Brockton, Massachusetts, says the term was created by her four-year-old daughter.

Muke. Strings of saliva in a speaker's mouth after drinking milk. Something that tastes *mukey* is something that gives off a mucilage aftertaste, such as is familiar with drinking cold milk in hot weather. (Stephen V. Masse, Amherst, Mass.)

Munge and **Farleyooge.** From the source: "These two words are the direct result of adding a baby (with a soft head) to a family with a delighted older brother and sister. The first word means to rub something (baby's head) affectionately, but vigorously. The second word describes the act of walking around a seated baby in a circle with one's hand on baby's head." (The Roussos family)

Mungodunno. Liquid of unknown origin and properties found in a jar or bucket. Usually discovered in garages or workshops, but can show up in refrigerators. (Stephen Haase)

Murgatroid. A proper name (at last) for those shiny, garden spheres that sit on pedestals in gardens. (Jennifer Morrison, Augusta, Me.)

Murphetic. That which conforms to Murphy's law, for instance, the fourth wheel on a shopping cart is usually murphetic. Some days are murphetic in the extreme. (John Clark, San Francisco)

Musgos. Leftovers and other food that "must go." Reported by a whole bunch of families. Sometimes *Mustgos*, *Mustgoes*, or *Muskos*. (KMOX, KNBR, WAMU, WHO, and more than a dozen letters)

Such a purging of leftovers seems to be a common event in American households. *Geriddas* is a dish of leftovers in the Konwiser family of Brick Town, New Jersey. It comes from such lines as, "I must get rid of this. I must get rid of that." *Take no prisoners night* is a time for using leftovers and throwing away all that is not eaten. (Barbara Gerovac, APO, N.Y.) And *catstinginingions* [cat-sting-in-ing-yons] in another family is a meal that often uses catsup and onions in addition to the leftovers. (Michael Ray, Collinsville, Conn.)

Muttney. Ever since *mutiny* was mispronounced by a member of this family, this has become a generic name for any badly mispronounced word.

Mutz. To pout or sulk behind closed doors, such as, "So now I suppose you'll go to your room and mutz." From Abbe Krissman of Glendale, Wisconsin, who points out: "I had always thought it was Yiddish, but no one else has ever heard or used it, so I guess someone in my family must have made it up at some point."

—NARROWBACK—

Nadia. Dinner is ready; come and eat. "In 1976 when Nadia Comeneci was a household name, come and eat sounded like Comeneci so our family just started calling Nadia, when everything was ready to eat. We still use it," say Mary Baeb of Oneida, Wisconsin.

Nancy. (adj.) Horribly perfect and goody-goody, usually applied to people. Inspired by *Nancy Drew*. (Linda Kent, Cambridge, Mass.)

Narrowback. A person not meant for heavy work. In Frank O'Hara's family it was applied to second generation Irish who, unlike their fathers, were not meant for hauling bricks. The late Ed Sullivan was a quintessential narrowback.

Naul Pewman. A handsome man who knows he's handsome. Derived, of course, from the name *Paul Newman*.

Nearsturtiums and **Farsturtiums..** "While traveling in Ireland," writes Sue Crawford of Coraopolis, Pennsylvania, "I was eager to learn all I could about the country. Our bus driver Paddy was a fountain of information about his homeland. I asked him about some flowers growing in the countryside. 'Oh, those here are nearsturtiums, and those over there are farsturtiums,' he explained with a straight face. After that, anything growing nearby was a nearsturtium, and anything growing far away became a farsturtium."

Neb. To pry, to thrust oneself in where one is not needed and not wanted, to mix into other people's affairs. (A word picked up in Pennsylvania and reported in the 1908 *Atlantic* article on Improvised Words. The word shows up later in Ivor Brown's *No Idle Words* as a Yorkshire word.)

Nephrotyte. A person who looks good but does nothing. (WIND)

Nerbils. Pieces of junk that accumulate in the sheets at the bottom of the bed. (Christine M. Short, Concord, Vt.)

Nerd. "My son and I are builders," writes John A. Main of Yorba Linda, California. "In addition to the popular concept of the term, we use it to describe those lumps of debris mixed in the paint which have to be sanded off before papering, the rough saw-cut edges of a board, and the ragged edges of sheetrock resulting from a cut by a dull razor blade knife."

Nerky. A blend of *nerd* and *jerky* that was created in one household to describe one particularly misshapen, ill-fitting, and hence nerky, baseball cap. (WRC)

Neutron Bread. Dense, amorphous bread that fails to rise. From Gregory J. Cebelak of Skagway, Alaska, who says that the term came from an ill-fated attempt to make whole wheat bread that evoked comparison to a neutron star.

Niblings. Nieces and nephews collectively; siblings

once removed. (KGO) Rachael Barenblat of New York City says that *nephices* is a synonym for niblings.

Nicknocks. Automobile turn signals, from the sound they make. (Gwynne A. Laning, Glenside, Penn.)

Nifnaffy. Out of touch with reality—it can be applied to an idea or someone who doesn't act right, or is a little bit off. (WHJJ) It would seem that many, many families either have a pet word or a phrase to describe this "offness." These are, variously, people who are a few bricks short of a full load, not wrapped too tightly, half a bubble off of plumb, one quart low, or have one oar out of the water. Their elevators don't go to the top floor, or they have a few sheep missing from their flocks, play with fifty-one cards, drive with one wheel in the sand, have one goose flying out of formation, and have dip sticks that don't reach the oil.

99. Grandmother, from the fact that 99 percent of the time when the phone rings, she's calling. (Tia Karekson, Minneapolis, Minn.)

N.O.C.D. Not Our Class Dear. Used by the "very snobbish" family of Susan Pomeroy of Harpenden Herts, England.

The Noise. A spring doorstop screwed into a baseboard. The name comes from the distinct noise that is made when it is bent and let snap back. (Brad Whitlock, Raleigh, N.C.)

NoK. (No-K) The opposite of *OK*. So logical that it gets reinvented by kids everyday, along with other logical pairings like "higher the window" (to match "lower the window"). (Herbert Paper)

Noonie. Naked state that occurs when kids take off their clothes to put on pajamas. Highway workers who take off their shirts in the summer are, likewise, part noonie. (Margaret Drye, West Lebanon, N.H.)

Nosegay. Dried nasal discharge visible to another member of the family. Useful, because the word can be worked into conversation so that another family member will know they must check themself. (Jane Harrison)

Nose Paper. Any paper product soft enough to blow one's nose into, including facial tissue, toilet paper, kitchen paper, and napkins. From Caroline Bryan, who says it was adopted by a group of her college friends when a pedant in their midst pointed out that toilet paper wasn't Kleenex.

No-thank-you-helping. A little bit, usually applied to turnips and other less-popular vegetables. (Eve C. Holberg, Corning, N.Y.)

Nov Schmoz Ka Pop. Comic strip character Smokey Stover used to say this before Sputnik went into orbit. It has survived in several families as an ersatz bit of low-key swearing.

Numyert. Yogurt, specifically that which is fed to a child to the chant of "num, num, num."

Nunty. An object of poor design and worse taste, often a gift that cannot be thrown away for fear of offending the giver. Submitted by Dr. Charles Davies of Calgary, Alberta, who says that the term dates back at least four generations in his family. He adds, "If allegedly functional (e.g., a corkscrew made of seashells and inscribed "Greetings from Nova Scotia"), it does not work. Paradoxically, though shoddily made, nunties are indestructible. Airport gift shops sell nothing else.

Nurdle. The quantity of toothpaste squeezed on a toothbrush. Reported by several correspondents. One of them, Mary Ann Raimond of Boynton Beach,

California, suggests an explanation for its showing up in various places: "I believe it was coined by the ad-exec of a now-defunct toothpaste company called 'Vote.'" It is also used as a verb ("Honey, please nurdle my toothbrush while you're in the bathroom") and is spelled *knurdle* in some quarters.

— OAK —

Oak. To study for finals or a crucial exam, derived from a bit of old slang "sporting the oak" for "closing one's door to outsiders." An *acorn* is a noncrucial exam. One does not oak for an acorn.(Caroline Bryan)

Oatmeal Meat. In a June 28, 1983, news conference, President Reagan told reporters, "Someday let me give you my recipe for oatmeal meat. I thought it was a luxury when I was a kid." The next day the White House got calls asking for the recipe, which was not available, and several reporters attempted to uncover the recipe through sources in his native Illinois. Phyllis Chasanow Richman of the Washington *Post* drew a blank from most of the people she contacted, but the "best guess" came from an agricultural extension agent who thought it was a meatless meatball, common during the Depression, that had been named "oatmeal meat" by Nellie Reagan and her brood. If that is what it was, it was made with spoonfuls of cold, cooked oatmeal, which were rolled in soda cracker crumbs and fried in a small amount of fat until browned. An Associated Press report, however, quoted Guy Ames of the National Oats Co., who thought that the president was referring to a dish called *goetta* that could be made with either corn meal or oatmeal. Quoting the AP report, "Goetta is a mixture of lean ground meats, oatmeal, and seasonings. Cooked ingredients are shaped into loaves and chilled. Slices of the loaves are fried in hot oil and served with butter and syrup."

Obesities. Large dirty words. (Dorothy Topping)

Octopusian. Tentacular. Created spontaneously in a law school class by a man who finds many opportunities to apply it. (WRC)

Oddy-oddy. The cry that goes up in one family whenever someone spots the stamped printing on a new pair of socks. (Karen Sjolund)

Odoralls. Toddler's overalls, for obvious reasons. (Margaret Drye)

Oik. The webbed space between two fingers, with the largest oik appearing between the thumb and forefinger. (Eric Greb, Stirling, N.J.)

Old Maids. Unpopped kernels of popcorn at the bottom of the popper. Seems to have fairly wide usage, as does "maids" for the same thing. "We can tell a good-quality popcorn from a poorer one because there are few, if any, 'old maids' in the bowl," writes Ian Farber of Kamloops, British Columbia

A profile of popcorn man Orville "The Colonel of Kernels" Redenbacher in the October 21, 1986, *USA Today* revealed that he used this term, too; adding that at one point he tried using "lazy fellows" but it just didn't stick. The article also revealed that *bees' wings* was the Redenbachean term for "Sizable pieces of the kernel's husk, which can get caught between the teeth."

Olga. The act of using a bit of water to dissolve the food remaining in a recently emptied pot, and pouring the "resultant slurry" into someone's bowl. From Norma Daniel of Escondido, California, who says, "This word 'honors' our super-thrifty friend Olga, who was apt to do this with guests as well as with family."

One! Do it now, or else. Comes from a father's "counting to three." (Peg Manion, Palm Bay, Fla.)

143. I love you, from the letter count for I(1) love(4) you(3). First reported by Fred Levy of Stoughton, Massachusetts, who adds that it is a convenient way to express love when others are listening.

One Over Par. Sharon Grace of Islington, Ontario, explains this coded phrase: "I recently dated a guy who had a problem with keeping his nose clean. So, if we were out or in the company of others and his nose had something embarrassing in view, my code to him was this, obviously meaning 'bogey,' e.g., "One over par on the left side."

One Spit. Something that is "just plain dumb." Reported by Al Williams of Atlanta, who writes, "When I was sixteen and on a family outing at the Birmingham zoo, I got ahead of everyone and came upon the llama yard. A sign warned, 'Caution I Spit.' Well, the llama was speaking to me [through the sign], warning me that he spits. I mistook the 'I' for a 'One' and the rest of the family guffawed." Williams says that there have been many one spits in his family, including the time that his mother drove more than 150 miles to have the heater on her car fixed, only to find that she had forgotten to turn the fan on.

On the Arrow. Needing a haircut. Similarly, to have gotten a haircut is to be *off the arrow.* Barbara Markunas of Sandown, New Hampshire, picked it up from her father and later found out that it was a reference to the collars of Arrow shirts.

Onways. A coinage from Logan Pearsall Smith for

"the stories that in one's dotage one tells them much more than once." The repeated stories of old age.

Oobs. It started as a golfer's cry in a Rhode Island family to indicate a ball that had gone out of bounds, but subsequently came to mean to them anything that was unacceptable or not permitted.

Ootocks. Shoes and socks as a single unit, as in "Don't forget your ootocks." It originated with a child who could not say shoes and socks and has been used ever since. (Lisa Meredith, San Diego, Cal.)

Outrance. The opposite of entrance; an exit. (Jane Tesh)

o-Vanzetti. A rare example of the family suffix. It is from writer and teacher Richard Lederer, who wrote about family words in his syndicated "Looking at Language" column. "This construction goes back to my wife's and my graduate school days together when, for some obscure reason, we latched on to the Sacco and Vanzetti murder trial and made a suffix from the two names. Ever since, things have been 'neato-Vanzetti,' 'crumbo-Vanzetti,' or 'stinko-Vanzetti'—but only in the Lederer family."

Overdog. Logical antonym to *underdog*. Reported by several people, with at least one incidence in print. (Georgia Tech basketball coach Bobby Cremins quoted as overdog coach in the Washington *Post*, December 28, 1984.)

Overneath. Something that is both over and underneath. Examples: a sleeping bag, sheets, or pita bread. (Erica Brothers, 13, Dayton, Oh.)

Owees. Oversized double-yolked eggs. From the Petersen family of Brockport, New York, who have hens that lay owees. One imagines the name is taken from the hen's noisy reaction when laying such an egg.

— PANG - WANGLE —

PADAFAG. Gene Botkin of Beaufort, North Carolina, wrote to say that this is a word from his mother's childhood. "She grew up in a small Midwestern town that had a slaughter house. Several days a week a wagon from the slaughter house would haul the entrails through town to a dump site in the country, and it was usually followed by a group of stray dogs. Whenever a family member observed an unusual mess of filth or nastiness, it was called a PADAFAG, meaning it was enough to: Puke A Dog Away From A Gutwagon!"

Pang-wangle. Cheeriness under minor discomforts, a humorous optimism under small misfortunes. "I pang-wangled home in the rain." (Introduced in the article "Improvised Words" in *Atlantic*, November 1908.)

Paper Brains. Handwritten notes in the hands of a person who depends on them. The term emphasizes their importance. (Barb Hasty, St. Louis, Mo.)

The Part. The label on a baby's blanket. "Your child cries in the night and wakes you up because they can't find *the part*," explains Maryjane Bailey of

Concord, New Hampshire. *Rubbies*, according to Stephen E. Smith of Boone, N.C., is the satin edging around a blanket. The *sulky* (silky?) or *cold cloth* in a Missouri family. My son Alex called the especially smooth place where the two ends of the satin binding overlapped *The Spot*, and for years he could not fall asleep until he had found it with his fingers.

Pass the potatoes. Family code phrase to change the subject at the table. (Lois S. Appel, Romeo, Minn.)

P.B. Place back, a signal made when you leave a chair but wish to reserve it. (Debbie Steensland, Arlington, Wash.)

Pedha? (Always a question) The ultimate of the who, what, why, where, when, how, pedha group. It means any and/or all of the other six. (Janet W. Hook)

Peeb. Short for "Poor baby" in one family: it totally lacks any implied compassion. (WAMU)

Peedling. Any child above the age of two or three and up to and including seven or eight. Peedlings tend to be novices at whatever they take up. (Chris Barth, Bay Village, Oh.)

Pejorkey. The state of a person who has gone to bed with wet hair and wakes to find it sticking out in all directions. The word came from a man who talked in his sleep and, in the middle of the night, while still sleeping, asked his wife what pejorkey meant. The woman, Tracy Barrett of Nashville, could not get the word out of her head and one day found that it "fit" for the condition described.

Penn Station. This is what one family terms a child's misinterpretation of a famous line or phrase. It came from one youngster's recitation of "The Lord's Prayer" that contained the line "And lead us not into Penn Station." (The line also appears as a pun in Saul Bellow's book *Humboldt's Gift* in the

100

same paragraph as "Two is company, Three is a Kraut."

Another family reports that the same phenomenon is called a *Harold* at their house because of this: "Our father who art in heaven, Harold be Thy name." Other Penn Stations: "Land where the pilgrims pried," "Bells on cocktails ring" (from "Jingle Bells"), "I pledge my allowance to the flag," and this from the late John A. Main of Yorba Linda, California, who reported, "As a child my wife came home from Sunday School one day and recited, 'Onward Christian Soldiers, Marching as to war, With the cross-eyed Jesus, Leaning on the phone.'" An Ohio woman's daughter came to the dinner table and recited the story of the Lord "and his twelve opposums." The hymn "Gladly the Cross I'd Bear" became "Gladly the Cross-Eyed Bear" in still another.

Still another name for much the same phenomenon first appeared in the title of a book by the late Amsel Greene, called *Pullet Surprises.* It was about malapropisms encountered in the classroom and took its title from a high school student who wrote, "In 1957, Eugene O'Neill won a Pullet Surprise." With full credit to Ms. Greene, Jack Smith of the *Los Angeles Times* came up with his own collection of such gems in a book called *How to Win a Pullet Surprise.*

Pep or popped? Question used when coffee is being prepared in the evening to find out if the person wants pep (coffee with caffeine) or is popped (and wants it decaffeinated so they can sleep.) (Robert Falk, Atlanta, Ga.)

Pepper Talk. The silly way that pet owners talk when speaking for their pet. (From Elyce K.D. Santerre of Manhattan, Kansas, who says it is named for a favorite family pet.)

Pernundal. The transmission of a car with automatic transmission. It comes from the letters on the steering column PRNDL for Park/Reverse/Neutral/Drive/Low. "Our family has used this word ever since my dad was trying to teach me how to drive and he said to me to put 'it' in drive," writes Barbara Thompson of Minooka, Illinois, "I answered, 'Put what in drive?'"

The Peruvial We. The "we" that we use to mean *you.* When a doctor or nurse says "How are we this morning," or your spouse says, "We'd better get this garbage out," they are employing the peruvial "we." Created by Judy Thompson and a friend, who felt "peruvial" had the right all-purpose sound.

The Phantom. One of the most interesting special grandmother names culled from the Gagas, Monks, Beebars, Nannas, Meemas, and Muzes. Explained by the Philadelphia man who submitted it, "Because one of our grandmothers was irrationally deaf to normal conversation, yet apparently had the power to hear the refrigerator door opening from three blocks away, she was (and is still) known as the Phantom." (Harrison Boyle)

Phee-dee. Person with a doctorate; Ph.D. This appeared in *Verbatim* in a letter to the editors following Allen Walker Read's article on "Family Words" and was submitted by Michele W. Fletcher of New Haven, Connecticut. The letter read in part, "One Sunday morning, shortly after my family had moved from Boston to Knoxville, Tennessee, my mother announced to us that, according to the newspaper article she was reading, there were more *phee-dees* in Knoxville than there were in Cambridge, Massachusetts. When my father asked what on earth a *phee-dee* was, she was stumped, finally saying, 'You know, a phee-aitch-dee.' Needless to say, as a family that boasts three college professors, including my mother, we found this slightly foolish word uniquely appropriate and have adopted it as our own."

Akin to this was Conrad Aiken's coinage *Ph. Demon*, which he described as a somewhat derisive reference to "the typical pedantic fellows who write laboriously learned theses for a Ph. D."

Phlug. Pocket lint and/or belly-button lint. In other families it is known as *nuf-nuf, smngus, phnur, neimildorf,* and *meh-meh*, which you say through your nose.

Phuds. A good example of a neighborhood word. "As a child in western Pennsylvania," writes Chet Klingensmith of Jacksonville, Florida, "I would join the rural neighborhood group occasionally to build a fire for warmth, roasting hot dogs, corn or potatoes, or just for lookin'. The older members of the group admonished that everyone had to have 'phuds.' This rhymed with 'goods' and was an individual's share of the sticks, dried weeds, and dead branches for the fire."

Pichinker. Television remote control that makes a "pichink" sound when it is used to turn the set on or off. (Becky Sharp, Plainfield, Ill.)

Pididdle. See *Kerfunkle.*

PIGOWEE. From Jerald D. Pope, ". . . the ancient and honorable battle cry of the Pope family. It means, in Low Scottish, to run away. Modern usage has degenerated to a signal for locating other family members in airports, shopping malls, and other public places. Discretion must be used concerning its appropriateness in hospitals and finer restaurants."

Pingle. To appear to be very busy while not doing anything at all. "Pingling is most easily achieved at one's desk or in a messy kitchen," says Jane Harrison, who adds that this was her British mother's favorite word.

Pipimist. A foreign body in one's drink. "Father squeezed fresh orange juice every morning and strained it to get the pips out. Sometimes one eluded the strainer and got in someone's glass, and would be fished out with the comment, 'Here is a pip he missed.'" (Margo B. Schworm)

Planacea. A cure-all strategy. Plan + Panacea. Created many years ago by writer Leonard Bacon, who once complained that he had tried to use this in a book but the printer struck out the *l* in the page proof.

Plernscrabble. Ice cream that is beginning to melt and drip down the side of the cone, as in, "You have some plernscrabble." (Naomi Patterson, Topeka, who has no idea where the term came from.)

PLOM Disease. Short for the "Poor Little Old Me" illness. (WRC)

Ploop. The roll of fat that commonly appears after the holidays and *ploops* down over the belt. (WIND) A woman who heard this insisted that it was not a ploop but a *dunlap*, because it dun laps over your belt.

Plumbsous. Squared away; plumb. (CFOS)

Podle. [poe-dil] (V.) To stand first on one foot and then on the other, occasionally crossing the legs and exhibiting an expression of distress, as in "Mama! Johnny's podling! Better find a rest room fast!" (Mrs. William Bendel, Framingham, Mass.)

Pome. Any dumb poem written for family or friends. From Heidi Gustafson of Parker, Colorado, who goes on to explain, "It must be about the person it is sent to and usually contains one or more words which have been modified in some way so that they rhyme."

— THE RACCOONS
WERE HERE —

Rabbit, Rabbit! "Don't ask us where or why we picked it up, but it's not original with us," writes Warren Johnston, who reports that the expression is a cry that goes up on the first day of the month when one family member first meets another.

The raccoons were here. Announcement made when it becomes obvious that one of the children has, to use the euphemism of old, broken wind. (Norman Mark) If this sounds odd, another family reported *Barking Spiders* for the same phenomenon, while it is *Squeezing the Fox* in still another.

Rachel, Rachel. A memory that jumps across the screen of the mind. From the movie of the same title, which used the device of quick flashbacks to tell the main character's story. (Rich Tewell, Atlanta, Ga.)

Raspenarious. All-purpose negative adjective: ornery, contrary, tipsy, whatever. Only the most raspenarious among us would object to its use. (WHO)

109

Razzle. To let one's foot fall asleep, as in, "My foot razzles." (Terry Kibiloski, Scott AFB, Ill.)

Recaptoids. Tire-tread fragments that appear along the highway after they have blown off recaps. So named in a *New Yorker* "Talk of the Town" item on the various recaptoid types.

Revlacormia. Temporary red marks on skin that come from sitting on deck-chair webbing, lying on wrinkled sheets, and so on. From the brother of an elementary school teacher who got it from one of his pupils. The teacher deemed it the best homegrown word he had ever heard. See also *Brinkles.*

Rigger. Small shudder. (KMOX)

Ring-for-Mary. Any inconvienient job that one ends up having to do oneself. The term is for a fictitious maid who is always taking her day off. (Gillian and Steve Crabtree, North Vancouver, B.C.)

'Rios. Any dry cereal eaten by hand as a snack. Originally from Cheerios. (Peg Manion, Palm Beach, Fla.)

Rips. Coupons found in magazines and newspapers entitling the bearer to a small cash rebate. From rip-off. (Kelly L. Webb, College Station, Tex.)

Rissywarn. Family work that appears in Carl Sandburg's *Prairie Town Boy.* Referring to the old wood stove in the family home, he wrote, "At the stove end was a small oblong tank holding water warmed by the warm coals. At first we children called this, as Papa and Mama did, *the rissywarn.* When we learned it was a reservoir, we went on calling it *rissywarn* out of habit."

Robinson Crewsock. The one lonely unmatched sock that seems to show up in every load of laundry. (Marlene Aronow, Deerfield, Ill.)

Rocking. Describing a woman having her period. From Nancy Craig of New Hope, Pennsylvania, who says, "It came from my sister's habit of using the rocking chair violently for a few hours each month. Remember, in those days Midol and Pamprin hadn't been invented . . ."

Rooch. Anything rumpled or roughed up: "The rug is rooched; unrooch it." (Howard Channing)

Rowley. The knob on the back of the alarm clock that is pulled out to set the alarm. Bill and Virginia Cressey of Bethesda, Maryland, sought a name for this knob for years, and then, when they were driving through Rowley, Massachusetts, it dawned on them that the name fit perfectly. A family in Texas found that *sneck* worked for them, while a California man said it was *orkney*.

Rubber Husbands. One divorcee's term for those nippled, rubber pads that are used to get pesky jar tops to turn. Another name for the same pad is *Dominic Feeny*. This is from the Hinkley family of Hicksville, New York. They report that Mr. Feeny is a local politician who once during an election year handed out these pads, emblazoned with his name. "When a jar is difficult to open, we say, 'Go get Dominic Feeny' or 'Dominic Feeny to the rescue.'"

Rumpsprung. Said of a chair, sofa, or other piece of furniture which is showing signs of having been sat in too often. (KNBR)

Runaround. A particularly vicious hangnail that will, if pulled hard, run around the finger in an arc of blood-spurting pain. (KMOX)

— SAGG —

Safes. Seat belts. Derived from messages like "Buckle up to be safe." (Kathleen Keefe, Casper, Wyo.)

Sagg. To lounge, laze around, take it easy, do nothing in particular. To enjoy a good sagg. (Jean Scott Creighton)

Saturday is longer than Sunday. Code line to inform a woman that her slip is showing. There are a number of these useful lines, including *It's snowing south of here* and *Snowing down South,* which crops up with some regularity. A Texas reader recently wrote to "Dear Abby" to report that he worked the word *valley* into the conversation when his wife's plunging neckline exposed too much cleavage.

Scheitterei. [sheet-er-eye] A noisy and/or chaotic event, usually family. An example from the family that claims it: "[We had] a real scheitterei when Baby Carol was discovered to have removed the stool from her diaper and smeared it over herself and the wall." Probable derivation is from that which tends to hit the fan.

Schnipples. Beyond any question, this word and its variations were reported more often than any other word. In each case it was reported as being a word peculiar to the family in question.

Judith Ann Hughes of League City, Texas, has written what amounts to a major definition, which is, in part, quoted here. "Schnipples are those little things that get all over the carpeting and can't be vacuumed up easily but have to be picked up by hand and put in the trash. Schnipples appear after someone has repaired a small appliance at the dining room table, for example, or after the dog, after playing in the empty lot, has been let in, or after the kids have done anything at all with scissors. Other schnipple-promoting activities include folding laundry, sewing, cleaning out a drawer, eating popcorn (even if carefully confined to the kitchen), or anything at all adults do with scissors.

"Schnipples mysteriously appear in the living room right before company arrives, even though you've vacuumed thoroughly and have not allowed kids or pets near the area. Or, after your guests have already arrived, you notice out of the corner of your eye a schnipple, which you were certain was not there five minutes ago. You surreptitiously remove it the next time you get up to serve coffee."

Lynn Kelley of Reno traces back the word *snipple* (with the same meaning as schnipple) four generations in her family. Ellen Gald of Viroqua, Wisconsin, grew up with *pritzel,* meaning the same thing as schnipple. She first learned it was a family word when she was helping to decorate her high school gym for the prom and told everybody to stay and help pick up the pritzels. "What had been chaos was instant silence as all eyes turned to me and the English teacher said, 'Pick up the *what?*' I tried to

113

explain but it was a hopeless situation. How do you explain 'family words' to non-family?"

Schnozzle-bone. Nose in one family that began to use it years ago when it showed up in one of the late Walt Kelly's *Pogo* comic strips. (KGO)

Kelly was a gold mine for this kind of innovative language. One contributor, John A. Main, came up with a list of his favorites including: *kidneygarten, labbertory apparatomus, brinery deep, fourthwidth, preezoom, clumber out, gummint projeck, infathomabobble, cannibalistics, elephront, boneafried, poison ivories, horribobble, astronominy,* and *mother goosery rinds.*

Scotton. A technique that replaces anger with sweetness and light. Taken from the name of a scotton practitioner named Jim Scotton and reported on in an essay in the *Christian Science Monitor* by Joan Baum that appeared on June 2, 1983. Baum further explained, "The Scotton takes its origin from a sense of righteousness, but its essence is awareness of the value of suppressing moral outrage and substituting instead, subtle response. . . . Doing a Scotton means using guile in place of fury, opting for effective action over emotional release."

Scringe. The logical mating of syringe and cringe to create an apt new name for the needle. (Jeanne Zieman, Vancouver, Wash.)

Scrowger-owger. Tack-extractor or claw on a hammer. (Colin Howard)

Scubble. Any large piece of equipment that is used to build roads. "The scubbles are holding up traffic." From Edie Danieli of Suncook, New Hampshire, who believes it came from steam shovel.

Scummenoya. Someone indulging in antisocial actions: "I wish those drunk scummenoyas would stop drag-racing up and down the street." Also, an interjection: "When the mess sergeant asked me to clean out the grease pit with my bare hands, I shouted *Scummenoya*." Ivan Martin and his wife created this word in 1952 to fill a void in daily conversation. They also use *scummenoid* as an adjective.

Scurve. Combined form of "What's the score? and "Whose serve is it?" Developed through badminton, but applicable to tennis, volleyball, ping pong, and so forth.

Scuzbum. That which remains at the drain of the bathtub after the water has left. (Michael Kaye)

Seattle. During a time of great difficulty the husband in this family had a dream that he would be offered a fantastic job in Seattle. It was only a dream, but the name *Seattle* became a byword for optimism and the fact that things would improve. It is used whenever the goings get tough. The family, now prospering, has a boat named Seattle.

Sejole. A meld of *seduce* and *cajole* from Boston radio personality Paul Benzaquin.

Selugi. A neighborhood word that pops up in and around New York. Robert Chirico defines it from his recollection of childhood, "One child, usually a bully, pulls the cap or other personal garment from another and tosses it back and forth to a group of accomplices. The game begins when one shouts 'selugi,' and it ends when the hat is retrieved or a meddlesome adult breaks it up."

Semi-opaque Marking Medium. An Army man once told the rest of his family that this is the official military name for a magic marker. Now everybody goes out of their way to say things like, "Could you hand me the orange semi-opaque marking medium?" (The same man notes that *random calculator* is Pentagonese for dice.) (WRC)

Sesquelingual. Short of bilingual, said of a person who speaks one language well and "gets by" in a second. It is an extended family word used by a group of English-speaking intellectuals living in the middle of French Quebec. (George Englebretsen, Lennoxville, Que.)

17B. Current in the family of Joseph E. Badger of Santa Claus, Indiana, who reports, "Any time I start to tell a story, one of my kids will say '17B.'. . . This is to suggest that I'm getting forgetful in my old age, and have told the same stories so often that they are numbered, similar to the joke of the man in prison who hears various inmates yell out only the numbers of different jokes printed in the prison's only copy of a joke book."

Sheba. Something acquired to create envy.

Sheriff's Badge. A gift for someone else that you really want for yourself. "My older brother inadvertently brought this into use when he was five years old," writes Kathy Enders of Langley, B.C. "He bought my Dad a Father's Day gift that consisted of a cap pistol, whistle, and sheriff's badge because he just *knew* how much Dad would enjoy them."

Shobun. The term invented on the spot by a teenager to describe the outfit of a Sumo wrestler seen on television. (WIOD)

Shondalay. Anything that is particularly large for its kind, for example, "Take that peach, it's a shondalay." (Dana Gilbert Craft, Albany, Ga.)

Shopwinding. Strolling along; 50 percent window shopping, 50 percent gabbing. From Doris P. Wipert of Columbus, Ohio, who adds, "In 1936 my high school girl friend got her tongue tangled and said [shopwinding] inadvertently."

Show Towel. One family's term for a guest towel. "Show towel" is a more accurate name since guest towels are never, ever used, even by guests." (Stewart Kaufman, Garrett Park, Md.)

Sideburns. Burnt pieces of scrambled eggs that stick to the vertical sides of frying pans. (Florence J. Ring, White Plains, N.Y.)

Sinus Friction. Any show or movie with lots of artificial special effects. It began with a child's mispronunciation of science fiction. (Peggy Keller, Honolulu, Hawaii)

64. Signal that one cannot speak openly—such as during a phone conversation when others are present—and want only to be asked questions that can be answered with yes or no. This appeared in a letter from Sylvia Gillis of Eugene, Oregon, in a July 1986 "Dear Abby" column on family words and codes.

Skips and Wind Pudding. One family's answer to the age-old question, "What's for dinner?" (Carol Andresen)

Sklass. Short for Sunday school class, used simply to save time when distinguishing sklass from regular school. (Betrenia Bowker, Kansas City, Mo.)

Sky Hook. One of a number of family "runarounds"—that is, objects kids get sent out to find but that don't exist. These appear to be borrowed directly from the military, where for generations recruits have been sent off to find skirmish lines, tent stretchers, cannon reports, mail buoys, and fresh water wrenches.

Slatch. A break, a time out. A variation on an old, seldom-used New England application of the word, meaning a piece of good weather in the midst of an otherwise stormy period.

Smeen. Facial expression between a *smirk* and a *smile*; applied to the phony smile of politicians. From radio personality Joel Spivak, who says it is not his word but he uses it anyway.

Smib. Cigarette burn on a bathroom wall. Part of a

collegiate attempt to promote a new word. (KNBR)

Smiling the boy fell dead. A family catch-phrase that appeared in John Duffie's column on family words in the *Monday* magazine of Victoria, B.C., for April 9, 1982. Quoting Duffie, "A friend of mine in Toronto once told me that whenever an apparently insoluble problem arises in his house, someone will invariably murmur, 'Smiling the boy fell dead.' The words, I learned, are from a poem that Robert Browning wrote, apparently on one of his off days, called *Incident of the French Camp.* It describes the heroic efforts of a very young soldier to deliver a message to his commander through the battle lines, and finishes this way:

> 'You're wounded!' 'Nay,' the soldier's pride
> Touched to the quick, he said:
> 'I'm killed, Sire!' And his chief beside,
> Smiling the boy fell dead!"

Smitwitifs. Word created from the SMTWTFS on all calendars. It is, to one child at least, a very important calendar word, as it appears on every page. (The Petersens, Rockport, N.Y.)

Snack Pockets. Side fat; "love handles." (WIND)

Snerzy Glopwat. [snert-zee GLOP-watt] *Deliberately* mixed up or randomized, for example, mixed-up vegetables are snerzy glopwat vegetables. (Tom Gill)

Snick. Droplet of saliva expelled while talking. (KMOX)

Snirt. Snow with dirt showing through. (KTRH)

Snoast. A mound or pocket of snow that persists into summer. Appropriately from Gregory J. Cebelak of Skagway, Alaska.

Snoke. Sneaking a smoke. From Betrinia Bowker of Kansas City, in whose family several members are trying to quit smoking and where suspicions of snoking are not uncommon. It began with an excited brother-in-law who discovered a backslider and shouted, "Aha! You've been sneaking a snoke!"

Snorkle. To laugh so hard that one's nose runs and gurgles. (C. Bryan)

Sowie. The dark area under the porch. (Virginia Cressey)

Specdents. The marks on the upper bridge of the nose caused by eyeglasses. (Mark Gloor, Lincoln, Neb.)

Speed-wrenched. Hasty, shoddy work. Based on an old line about pliers being called "speed wrenches" by workers too lazy to select the proper-sized wrench. (Marshall T. Baker, Corona, Cal.)

Splot. Term for batteries that are all almost dead. Using splot batteries in a toy car means that it will not go very far or fast. (Christine Tiffany, Memphis, Tenn.)

Spluttergut. A highly excitable and/or emotional person. The kind you would least like to be stuck with in a stalled elevator. (Ben Willis)

Spock. "Draw your lips in between your teeth," writes Bob Thurston of Tallahassee, Florida. "Now try to suck in some air without opening your mouth. Now—quickly—open your mouth. It's just like kissing (pecking), except you've retracted your lips. That's a spock. It's how my Dad used to kiss us goodbye on his way to work each day. Our day was shot from the start if we didn't get spocked." (In my family a spock is a *mwah*.)

Spoon Hug. A hug made from behind (because the bodies nest like spoons). (Debbie Paliagas, Chippewa Falls, Wis.)

S.P.S.. Self-Praise Stinks. (Lena Cole)

Squaze. What a sponge does after it has been

squeezed; a sponge exhaling. Invented by Mildred Shapiro's kids about twenty-five years ago. A sponge became a *squeezy-squaze.*

Squirk. *School* + *Work.* The word was created by a woman who tired of making distinctions when asking members of her family if they had packed lunch for school or work. (Cathy M. Clark, Fort Walton Beach, Fla.)

Squitters. Little puddles left by puppies and kittens. (CFQC)

Stainful. Characteristic of such things as shoe polish, grape juice, spaghetti sauce, and ink. Also applied to certain ill-starred articles of clothing like yellow neckties and white slacks. (Margaret Atwood, who adds, "Mothers *need* this word.")

Starters and Stoppers. "When traveling abroad, one is liable to get either constipation or diarrhea, or (sequentially) both. So the wise traveler goes to the doctor beforehand and gets two prescriptions, one for Starters and one for Stoppers, to handle either contingency," says Margo B. Schworm.

Stewp. A meal served in a bowl which is thicker than soup and thinner than stew. (Cathy Voss, Morrison, Mo.)

Stick-togethers. Oreos and other filled cookies. (M.A. Lange)

Streely. Stringy unkemptness, such as that which comes to thin curtains that have hung too long, one's hair after a particularly busy day, some beards and old bathrobes. (Reported in the 1908 *Atlantic* article on Improvised Words)

Strodie's Pig. A spectre invoked for anyone who is overeating; usually called up in the line, "Remember Strodie's Pig!" It appears in Kim S. Garrett's "Family Stories and Sayings" and has been in her family since the 1860s, when a pet pig died from overeating, or, as it was sometimes called, "busted from too much buttermilk." See also "Weather to bring the stock into the parlor," from the same article.

Stroinke. [stroyn-key] Stretching your toes as far apart as you can, after having just removed them from shoes that don't fit. "AHHH! Stroinke." From Renee Charles of Green Bay, Wisconsin, who included instructions for its use: "The proper way to do it is to raise your feet in front of you and say it aloud as if it wouldn't help any if you didn't."

Stroom. To place one's tongue in the side of one's cheek, thereby causing a prominent lump. "She stroomed to keep from laughing." From a Detroit man, who said that his father got the word from a pre-World War II issue (December 3, 1938) of *Life* magazine but he never again found it in print. (WXYZ) A check on the files at the Merriam-Webster Company, which has collected some 13 million citations on words and their usage, shows that they had but one reference to the word from *Life*. It was used in a picture of a football coach who was strooming.

One can only guess that either a *Life* caption writer had unwittingly introduced a family word into his copy and it was not challenged, or it was a bold attempt by a group at the magazine to slip a new word into the language. In any event, that single mention was enough to keep it alive in one family for more than forty-five years.

Stroonge. To pour very hot coffee or tea back and forth between two cups to cool it off—"I can't drink it that hot, it's got to be stroonged." (Barbara L. Brown, Concord Township, Oh.)

Strucklogue. Lint or other foreign particle that appears on one's clothing. (KNBR)

Suculate. To squish Jell-O back and forth through your teeth. From Virginia Pastoor of Greenville,

Michigan, who asks: "Why do so many kids prefer plain Jell-O without any fruit in it?" The obvious answer, "It suculates better." She adds, "My kids made it up. Or they pulled it out of some collective childhood subconscious where it had been lying unused."

Suffonsify. To satisfy sublimely. Expressed in the line, "My sufficiency is suffonsified." (Jeremy Burr) In another family, *surresify* is used for the same state of well-being, and in still another extra portions are turned down with "No, thank you. I've had a genteel senuffency and a diabolical complenty." One is "totally farctated" in my wife's family, and the ritual in a friend's home is, "No, thank you, I have had a gentle sufficiency. Anymore would be a redundancy obnoxious to my system."

Sunday Bag. This is a better class of paper bag, to be saved for use on Sundays or holidays when bringing food or gifts to other people's houses. The Chicago lady whose family uses the term says that a supermarket bag is for everyday, but one from Marshall Field and Co. is a Sunday bag. (WIND) Marion Lehuta of Montgomery, Alabama, writes in a similar vein to report that in her family "two or more matching Goldblatt's Department Store shopping bags" are called *Matched Luggage.*

Suppertash. Common family version of the word *succotash.*

Swears. Nasty words. Created by young Elizabeth Thorpe of North Haven, Connecticut.

S.W.U.D.. Small, White, Ugly Dog. Generic name for toy poodles, pomeranians, and other small dogs. (Bill H. Whitton, Williams Lake, B.C.)

Symwyc. (simm-wick) Short for Shut Your Mouth When You Chew, as in, "Johnny's not symwycing." (Mrs. Fred Terry, Clarkston, Ga.)

— THANK-YOU · MA'AM —

Taking one of nature's cuts. Falling asleep in front of the TV. Cited as a family word on the BBC's "My Word." See also *Vidozer*.

Taney. Penis, in the family of Roberta Kraft of Washington, D.C., who adds, ". . . you can imagine how shocked and giggly I was when I learned the Supreme Court Justice in the Dred Scott decision was Roger Taney (I later learned it was pronounced 'Tawney') of Maryland."

Tarmac. (V.) To sit in a fully loaded aircraft for an extended period of time. Used by Senator John C. Danforth of Missouri on National Public Radio, March 16, 1987.

Teetulinear. (1) Very small (used mostly for inanimate objects); (2) In a frenzy. From the nickname of a pet dog belonging to David Mumper of Concord, New Hampshire.

Tenile. [with a long "e" at the beginning to rhyme with senile.] Condition of people having middle-aged crises, complete with mood swings, affairs, job changes, and so forth. Created by Judy Thompson, who says of the word, "Since it does seem to be a second-adolescence, I just combined the two extremes, teenage and senile."

Thank-you-ma'am. A pronounced rise and fall in the road that gives a roller-coaster-type thrill in a car going over 40 mph. These were once common almost everywhere but are now largely confined to asphalted back roads in the country. (Warren Johnston)

Thig. A fat thigh. (Created by dropping the final -h) (Gayle Grove, Hagerstown, Md.)

Through-leaves. Victoria Sackville-West, the English author, said in a radio talk that her family used this expression to describe life's most pleasurable moments. It was because, as children, they loved shuffling through the very dry, very brown leaves in autumn. "It was definitely a through-leaves experience." (Recalled and reported by Ross Reader)

Thumper. Disdainful cry when a very simple question shows up in Trivial Pursuit. It was created from the answer to this question: "What was the rabbit's name in Bambi?" (Jean M. Ogden, Abbotsford, B.C.)

Thunder Jug. Chamber pot, according to a Maine woman in her late seventies, who says that when she was a girl there were all sorts of names for this important object, including whistle pitcher, thunder mug, and po'.

Thwathy. Describes the taste and feel of a piece of fruit which is supposed to be juicy but turns out to be flannel-like. (Sally O. Davis, New London, N.H.)

Tim. Notation at the bottom of a typed page where the typist usually initials the letter. In this case, though, it stands for "typed it myself." (On a letter from Wanda Sanborn, High Falls, N.Y.)

Time for the blue fairy to fly. Said when the garbage

needs to be taken out. From Dorothy E. Tompkins of Knoxville, Tennessee who suggests that there must be many colorful, family code phrases for this ripe moment. (Friends refer to it as *Going to Dr. Bird,* because they used to put their garbage in a dumpster belonging to Dr. Bird.)

TMBF. A rating in a family with small children who are not allowed to see movies that are rated TMBF (for Too Many Bare Fannies). (Teresa Cornelius, Industry, Ill.)

Toad Cloth. Any dishrag that has gotten too wet and clammy to dry dishes. (Jane Tesh, Mt. Airy, N.C.)

Tod. Awkward, heavy, bashful; socially backward.

The word appears in the aforementioned article on Improvised Words in the *Atlantic*. The author had heard it applied to "a rather stodgy, embarrassed presence at a lively party of young people in a very lively little city of Maryland." The author added, "The more I thought about it, the better I liked it; 'tod'—it does sound dull and heavy, doesn't it? But I believe the use of it in that sense is confined very closely to that particular locality, for nowhere else have I heard it."

Tofu. Total fool. The word came from a misunderstanding of a woman volleyball player who kept calling herself a total fool when she missed the ball or ran into a teammate. The woman in question, Alicia DiDado of Culver City, California, reports that a friend asked her why she kept calling herself a "tofu," and the new meaning of the word was launched.

Tomorning. Tomorrow morning. (Clayton W. Yoho)

Toolicious. Extra delicious. (WIOD)

Tooth Twine. Term used by Katherine White for dental floss. Before he died, E.B. White said that the term was the creation of his late wife, Katherine, and that the first time he heard her use the term, "I knew that a girl who called dental floss 'tooth twine' was the girl for me." This story was recounted in Ralph Keyes's article on family words in *Good Housekeeping* magazine.

Torticulear. In a slow manner, such as that of a tortoise. (Enok Lohne, Dos Rios, Cal.)

Tote-bag Hell. Ever since Tom Shales of the Washington *Post* used this in his television column it has become the phrase in our house to describe those periods when the local public television station schedules those interminable "pledge breaks."

Totism. Word or phrase uttered by children within the range of two to six years that is hysterical when they say it, but if an older child were to say it, it would be stupid or offensive. From Jon Fasman, twelve, of Rockville, Maryland. It is his word and definition.

Tremense. That which is bigger than a four-year-old. (Frederic W. Gill, Shaker Heights, Oh., who learned it from his daughter Sara)

Troll. A Michigander who lives below the Mackinac Bridge (from the creatures that live below bridges), as opposed to one on the upper peninsula of Michigan, who is called a *Yopper*. (Jim and Jules Michelini)

Trolley. When a dog drags his bottom along your lawn or, more likely, your rug. "Look out, she cried, Puzzy's about to trolley on the new carpet." (Colin Howard)

Tulokat. That which cannot be touched—something "to look at." (KGO)

T.T.I. Short for Tummy Tuck-In, what one woman's mother asks to be told when "her middle-age middle begins to relax." (Diantha Thorpe.)

Turkey Letter. Any letter that is too wordy or too

long. This came from a young bride who wrote to her mother in a distant state asking for a recipe for a traditional holiday meal. Her mother was careful not to omit the smallest detail, and replied with handwritten directions on bird selection, stuffing, and roasting, which covered t*w*enty pages. (Alice L. Deal, Myrtle Beach, S.C.)

Tuskers. The elderly. It was reported by a man who first heard it at a Florida rest home and now uses it as a term of honor for the old "elephants" of society. (WRC)

Twangle. To twist and tangle. (Ruth Kingsley, from her late daughter Joan Kingsley Wheeldon)

Twater. Water set out to boil for hot tea; tea water. (Nita Denny, Manning, S.C.)

Twiller. A good looking, perhaps rather raffish, young man. (Terence Blacker, London.)

Twinition. A term to describe the special intuition shared by twins, such as buying the same birthday card for each other. (Deb Miller, an identical twin, Kent, Oh.)

Twinsy. Way of treating twins that is exemplified by dressing them identically. "I didn't give them twinsy names" is the way the mother of twins used the term in a report on twins on "Good Morning, America" on August 3, 1983.

TWN. *That which nothing*, as in "That which nothing could be better or worse than." It is used at the end of a sentence, such as "She served roasted bulbs of garlic in chocolate sauce, TWN." John Clark of San Francisco says that TWN has been used in his family for more than a hundred years, but debate still rages over whether it is pronounced "twin" or "toon."

Two-toes. Rubber beach thongs. From Martha Sandman Holmes of Oakland, California, who adds this charming bit of information on this family word: "When my father became president of an international trade association, he toured all over the country speaking to different groups. In San Francisco, he gave a speech and mentioned how he wanted to put on a bathing suit and two-toes and go to the beach! I was there and realized that probably no one there understood what he was talking about, except my mother and myself."

(Ironically, it was not until hearing this story that it dawned on me that the term *go-aheads*, which my family, and my wife's before that, used to call "two-toes," was, if not a strictly family term, less than universal. Since then I have been asking friends what these rubber thongs are called in their homes, and they have given me these answers: *holders, come-alongs, flip-flops, slappers, zorries, flippers, foot-os, Jesus slippers, and JC's.*)

Twupguttem. John Duffie, who writes the Overset column for *Monday* magazine in Victoria, B.C., brings this to our attention: "H. Allen Smith's *Low Man Rides Again* contains a wonderful expletive that Smith used under trying circumstances. Whenever he saw or read about an overly rich person doing something outrageous or stupid or both, he would mutter 'Twupguttem,' which was as close as he could come to pronouncing the acronym TWPGTM, or 'The Wrong People Got The Money.' John McEnroe makes me say twupguttem frequently."

— UFFISH —

Uffish. Blend of *uppish* + *selfish*. An oddity in that it is a family word from a novel discovered by Allen Walker Read. Compton Mackenzie's 1926 novel *Fairy Gold* is about a family living an isolated life on a small island off the coast of Cornwall. The children use a number of blends in talking with each other, including uffish, *glumpy* (*gloomy* + *grumpy*), and *sloach* (*slow* + *coach*).

Charles F. Dery points out that *uffish* appears in Lewis Caroll's *Jabberwocky*. The title character is described "as in uffish thought."

Uglies. Homework. This evolved from homework, to homely work, to the aptly disdainful, uglies. (Mrs. Thomas Palek, Los Gatos, Cal.)

Ummer. A live-in partner of the opposite sex, derived from the problem encountered when introducing such a person, "I'd like you to meet ummmm . . .er." From a 1983 article in the *New York Times* by Helen Jarvis McReynolds entitled "Some Straight Talk on 'Boomerangs.'" But it appeared earlier in Herb Caen's column in the San Francisco *Chronicle* and has appeared elsewhere (as either ummer or ummm) since then, such as in a 1986 article in *Newsday* by Marilyn Goldstein entitled "Ummm's the Word—for now."

Underfootage. Standard condition prevailing when cats are in the kitchen. "There is a considerable underfootage of furry beasts!" (Margo B. Schworm)

Undy-gundy. [oondy-goondy] Marks left on your ankles by your socks. (Vicki Ward, Sharon, Pa.)

Unihorn. Unicorn, aptly renamed by a youngster. This appeared in a continuing collection of examples of "family lingo" that appeared in the weekly column of Walter Berkov, book editor of the Cleveland *Plain Dealer* in the spring of 1985. It all started with Berkov recalling a term that had survived from the time when his daughter Ellen was a tyke—*oopiebites* for soup—and he asked for other words that had survived childhood. Most were restatements on the order of *unihorn.* Other examples from Berkov's collection as well as others submitted individually:

All rotten taters = Au gratin potatoes

Awfuls = Waffles (especially when they stick to the pan)

Basedump = Basement

Beanzilponts = Brussels sprouts

Butterflags = Butterflies

Chewcumbers = Cucumbers

Corn on the bone = Corn on the cob

Cowboy house = Ranch-style home

Dough-ring = Doughnut

Flumb = Thumb

Flutterby = Butterfly

Gush-gush maker = Food processor

Hand motion = Hand lotion

Helichopters = Helicopters
Icydangles = Icicles
In the communicado = Incommunicado
Keppitch = Catsup
Legotards, Legtards = Leotards
Lickstick = Lipstick
Oogret = Yoghurt
Orepot = Airport
Round-a-round = Ferris wheel
Scalped potatoes = Scalloped potatoes
Scumuitoes = Mosquitoes
Skeetemo bite = Mosquito bite
Smashed potatoes = Mashed potatoes
Uppoobah, Rainbrella, Unclebrella = Umbrella
Windshipper, Windshopper, Whipshield wiper, Windsweeper, Whipwipers, Wind sticks, Winchell wipers = Windshield wiper
Yunyuns = Onions

Unobtanium. Substance or item that is needed but that does not exist or cannot be found. A family word in that it was used by the pioneers in the early days of the U.S. space program.

Upbringingcy. The state of upbringing, as in the oft-heard family question, "Have you no upbringingcy? (WAMU)

Upper-gotchee. Brassiere. (Ann Marie Willer, Carrollton, Tex.)

Upscuddle. An argument. "They had a big upscuddle about it." (Garrett Riggs)

Uster. A child's chair that has been in the family for four generations, so called "because many years ago a small child said his Mommy uster sit on it." (Jean Wheatly, Grants Pass, Ore.)

Utubious. Self-evident, obvious. "The answer should be utubious to the most casual observer." The word, says Ashley H. Steele of Toledo, Ohio, who reports it, originated as a misprint in an MIT text entitled *Radar Theory and Practice* and "has been part of my vocabulary for twenty years." He has had no trouble with the word as no one dares ask what it means.

Utz. To push a person's psychological button, from a friend of Joann Lee. "I really utzed him by saying how much he sounded like his brother." It is also the button itself.

— VANCHOCSTRAW —

V 'n' X. A generation-old term for the five-and-ten-cent store that started out as a pre-Christmas code word by adults. Now it is applied to any variety or department store. (WCKY)

Vanchocstraw. One family's considerable improvement over the name *Neopolitan* for a kind of ice cream. (KMOX)

Vegicrud. The unidentifiable organic matter that migrates to the far corners of the refrigerator's vegetable crisper section. (Marlene Aronow, Deerfield, Ill.)

Video Suppers. An elegant stand-in for TV dinners that has obtained in my family. Originally it came from the "Ritchie Rich" television cartoon show, on which the butler used the term to give class to the frozen dinner.

Vidozer. A person who tends to fall asleep during a television program. This word was sent in by a reader and appeared in John Crosby's column in the old New York *Herald Tribune* when commercial television was still in its infancy.

— W-PANTS —

W-pants. Pants that are too tight in the crotch; named for the shape they make from the front. (Debbie Paliagas)

Wanky. Lacking energy; describing a general feeling of lassitude. (An old family word from author Agnes Sligh Turnbull from the 1946 *Word Study* article on "Who Makes Up the New Words?")

Want-need. Double verb used to prevent a parent from saying, "You may want ice cream, but you don't need it." The child, anticipating the old ritual, simply says, "I want-need an ice cream cone." (Ruth Bayerle)

Warsaw. Injunction for "Be quiet"; a polite "Shut up." Reported by fourteen-year-old Catherine Marshall of St. Mary's, Pennsylvania, who says that it all started when she was very young and used to talk incessantly with her greatest powers coming on long car trips. On one particular five-hour trip, the family approached a town called Warsaw, and Catherine's father stated that children were not allowed to talk in this particular town. If they did, they would be arrested by chickens riding motorcycles. Before long, every other town was deemed to be Warsaw.

Weather to bring the stock into the parlor. This expression is explained by Kim Garrett in her article on "Family Stories and Sayings": "The saying dates to the storm of '86, when all the tribe sought shelter in Grandfather's stone house in Sutherland Springs. The family at that time included Telegraph, Uncle Alley's big white horse. Uncle Alley was badly crippled (a fact that Telegraph seemed to understand) and looked on his horse as a beloved companion as well as safe transportation. Telegraph was stabled on the porch at first, but as the storm grew worse, Uncle Alley grew more restless. No one thought it too strange when he asked that Telegraph be brought into the house. The parlor was the only room not crowded with kin, so Telegraph spent the rest of the night surrounded by family daguerreotypes and fancy antimacassars."

Wechsel. A lecherous male. "It originated during a vacation in Italy," writes Anna Berg of Deerfield, Illinois, "We were looking for a bank to exchange money. Spotting one, I pointed across the street, yelling 'Look, a *wechsel*,' which means exchange in German and was on the bank's sign. An eager man passing on his bike thought I was pointing at him, and came closer to ogle at me."

Weebs. Generic name for people over thirty who eat too much and exercise too little. Taken from the egg-shaped toy, Weebles, which have as their motto, "Weebles wobble but they don't fall down." (Nancy Stewart, Erie, Penn.)

Wha'-oh? Question asked after hearing a crash and a loud "Uh-oh!" from another room; short for, "What was that 'Uh-oh!' about?" (Susan McVey, Sunnyvale, Cal.)

Whats. A dessert of ice cream on donuts. According to W. Bryan Stout of Urbana, Illinois, this was created by his mother in despair after being asked once too often, "What's for dessert?" Henceforth, she could say, "Yes."

Whereas. A nitpicker, as in "He's a real whereas." From "Whereas the party of the first part, etc." From Margaret Atwood, who adds, "As I write this . . . I see that it could easily evolve into Whereass, and don't we all know some of them, too?"

While. Unit of time almost always expressed in the plural. "I'll see you in a couple of whiles." From Jane Harrison, who makes this important point: "This usage only works in a family where every one knows each other's comprehension of time. Obviously, six whiles is a longer period than two whiles, but it is not necessarily three times longer. In general, waiting whiles are longer than more active whiles, just as unpleasant whiles are longer than pleasant whiles."

White Clouds. The white foam that often forms at the corners of one's mouth after a tooth-brushing. (Mary Beth McGowan, Albany, N.Y.)

Whoopies. Bumps and small hills that when crested by a car cause your stomach to "drop." (Minnesota Public Radio) This rather enjoyable sensation evokes other terms from other families. The Carpenter family of West Melbourne, Florida, calls the sensation *tickle belly,* while *fluffy and hard* describe the way one's stomach feels, according to Tony Hess. Susan Austin of Wappingers Falls, New York, says her family calls the place where the dip occurs a *hauny hill.* Interstate highway systems and efficient state and local road departments are making whoopies more and more of a rarity.

Whooty. Expression of mild sympathy. "Ah, whooty!" (Peter DeWeese, Fairfax, Va.)

Wiffle. A case in which a family word became the name of a popular product. In his article on family words, "Family Spoken Here," Ralph Keyes pointed out that when young David Mullany struck out his playmates while playing stickball with a plastic golf ball, he claimed he had "whiffed" them. The ball was dubbed the "whiffle ball" and when David's father created a baseball-sized version, he dropped the "h" and capitalized the "w."

Wiggings. Scoldings, given by Queen Victoria to her family and government ministers. Rarely does a family word appear in the *Encyclopaedia Brittannica*, but this one does, showing up deep in the entry for "Victoria, Queen."

Wiggleyfon. The sheathed string on a hooded sweatshirt. (KNBR) Another family calls these shirtstrings *hoodwinks.*

Winky-winky. Code for sex when even hanky-panky was too direct. (Lori Schlichtori, College Point, N.Y.)

Winston Oaks. Any place that one keeps coming back to when lost. It comes from a real incident in which a family got lost and kept coming back to a sign that said "Winston Oaks." It is now applied to anything that one comes back to (a poem, a dish, an old friend) in terms of trouble and confusion.

Wishes. Dandelion seeds, which are blown off when wishes are made.

Wistow. Created and reported on in a letter from Neil Croll of Derby, England: "When my train passed Wistow the other week, the name became a word for a secret consolation, as when a bore (or drillig) has buttonholed you but only you know that your bus is coming."

Wixie Bones. Anything good—from cookies to toys. Term created and used by the son of Shaun Usher of Surrey, England.

Won't be noticed on a gallopin' horse. Said of barely

noticeable flaws in one's appearance, such as a spot on a blouse. (S. Clemens, Decatur, Mich.)

Wordo. Word collector. Ray Leedy of Mercer Island, Washington, was labeled as such by the late Richard von Hallberg.

Wudge. (1) A pile of clothes, (2) the appearance of a shirt or skirt after it has been sat on, and (3) a sleeve that comes out with an outer sleeve. (WIND)

— X.Y. Z —

X.Y.Z. This, used when an adult notes that a young man's fly is open in a gathering that goes beyond the immediate family, stands for Xamine Your Zipper. Like *F.H.B.*, *X.Y.Z.* appears to have broken out of the realm of just one family, since I have heard it from people in various parts of the country. An alternative is *B.U.* for Button Up, from a radio show call-in participant.

In the summer of 1986 a "Dear Abby" column was devoted to letters on X.Y.Z. and affiliated family codes. One of the most interesting was contained in a letter from Denise Biggins of Fairport, New York, who said, in part, "I'm an immigrant from the 'old country' and was brought up on Shakespeare. In our family, we'd say, 'Ah, woe is me'—the rest of the phrase, 'for I am undone,' was, of course, unnecessary."

— YABOTTS —

Yabotts. Any excuse or argument about to be made, derived from the "Yeah, but . . ." that so many of these statements start with. Most commonly used as "No yabotts" to forestall further discussion. (Tara Lawson, Burlington, Ont.)

Yalmulkettes. Specific name for the small bowl-shaped pieces of Styrofoam used as packing material. (Johnathan R. Hancock, Syracuse, N.Y.)

Yamoo. The best; that for which there is no equal; the real yamoo. (WRC)

Yard Ape. Overly active mischievous child who tends to do less damage outside than in. (Matthew and Daniel Sissman, Latham, N.Y.) On hearing of this term, Suzie Radus of Pittsburgh wrote to point out that the urban corollary to the suburban/rural yard ape is the *Porch Monkey*.

Yarden. The fragments of land that surround most of today's mortgages. Neither yard nor garden. From Bertram C. Cooper of Macon, Georgia, who got it from his then six-year-old grandson.

Yawn. Logical blend word produced by adding lawn and yard. (Carol Ohlson, Wataga, Ill.)

Yehoodi. In more than a few families, this was the name for an imaginary person who left the television on, didn't flush the toilet, or committed any of a number of other household sins. In his *Complete Unabridged Super Trivia Encyclopedia,* Fred Worth has an entry for "Yehoodie" which may explain its origin. It reads, "The little man who pushes the next Kleenex tissue up in the Kleenex box. As created by Bob Hope on his radio program." Worth also carries an entry for *Yehudi* that reads, "Non-existing character created on radio by Jerry Colonna. He's never heard or seen."

You know me, Eddie. In a column in the British *Competitors Journal,* Robert Kendal describes a number of family words and phrases but dwells on this one:

"A long-time friend of ours called Eddie Scott went to visit some relatives of his, a Welsh farming family, somewhere in the outback of Caernarvonshire. His car broke down and he had to spend the night.

"The only accommodation the family could offer at such short notice was the option of sharing a bed with Eddie's six-year-old nephew, Llewellyn. All went well until around four o'clock in the morning, when Eddie was awakened by an urgent thump in the back.

"'What's the matter?' he called sleepily, wondering where he was.

"Young Llewellyn, in the bed beside him was polite, but apologetic.

"'You know me, Uncle Eddie,' he said confidentially, 'I don't like to disturb you. But I thought I'd better tell you I've just wet the bed.'"

The phrase is used as the lighthearted preliminary to bad news.

Your Elephant. Said of a non sequitur or extraneous point, as in "That's your elephant." From Elizabeth Samuels of Scottsville, Viriginia, who got it from her daughter Amy, who was responding to her father's use of "That's irrelevant."

Yournotsam. Word created to cover the fact that you went fishing and caught nothing. It stems from a joke, according to Shirley Sax of Morton Grove, Illinois:

"When my daughter Linda went fishing and lost her only nibble, I told her the joke where two men go fishing every weekend. Sam catches his limit and Joe catches nothing. One day in frustration Joe says to Sam, 'Sam, this is aggravating. Next weekend pick your spot. Let me pay you $25.00. For a year we've gone fishing and I've caught nothing. I can't seem to choose the right place to pick from as you always do.' So Sam agrees and the following weekend out they go, Sam picks the spot, Joe pays him the $25.00, Joe casts into the lake and sure enough dozens of fish swarm around. Joe is thrilled until one looks up at him and says, 'You're not Sam!' and they all swim away."

You should see my aunt. One family's phrase in response to a dumb action. It came from a domestic servant who after a botched job had said, "If you think I'm dull, you should see my aunt." Reported in John Duffie's column on family words.

Yown-yowns. (rhymes with down-downs) Small crisp pieces of batter, the by-product of frying chicken. (Rebecca Rasor Freeman, Rockwall, Tex.)

Yulke. The little grains of dried secretion found in the corner of one's eyes in the morning. The man who gave me *yulke* told me that it had been used in his family for so long he thought it was a real word, and it wasn't until he was in the Army and used it that someone told him that it wasn't in the dictionary. (WIND)

Other words for *yulke: kitties, quick, glee, maggie, tapioca, overnights, kitty-kocky, dust bugs, sand, peepers, sleepers, sleepies, sleepie dots, speedies, eye cheese, eye boogies, bleach, sleep dirt, eye fat, dream dust, fump, crunchies, shrum, duck doodles,* and *duck feed.* (One suspects that the word "duck" shows up in some of these terms because a child was told that the secretion came from the tear ducts.)

— Z√ZZ1S —

Zep. Sudden confrontation with truth—e.g., the moment of zep. This is one of several words created by Stephen V. Masse of Amherst, Massachusetts, and his friends (Kyle Hoffman-Setka and Frank Jay) while playing "No-Word Scrabble." He explains the game, "One evening in desperation as the word possibilities grew slim, a friend and I began to make up words which had to sound like real words: After scoring all our letters, we decided to come up with definitions." *Zep* was one that seemed passable, as did

Achavy. Murder by snake. An *achavist* is the killer.

Ko. Insect manure.

Stensid. Extremely malodorous, stenchy, and rancid.

Thogrim. Mathematical certainty achieved by looking up the answer in the back of the book.

Whelg. An expired meteorite.

Zerbert. A "kiss" in which the kisser blows on the kissee's skin, producing an obnoxious but affection-

144

ate noise. The zerbert made its debut on a 1986 episode of *The Cosby Show.* (Not to be confused with *Blutz*, q.v.)

Zib. The sound of an acetate tab being pulled from the tape on a disposable diaper. (Minnesota Public Radio)

Zoned. Said of someone so strange that they seem to have come from out of the "Twilight Zone." (Nancy Dotson, Big Sur, Cal.)

Zsaj. To spiff up in the manner of Zsa Zsa Gabor. From a woman whose physicist husband wants to be dressed in red, blue, black and white, and no patterns. "Every once in a while I try to zsaj him up." (KMOX)

Zuzzis. The strong tingles in your foot when it falls asleep. (Anita Locke, Kensington, Md.)

Last Words

We need new words—and great ones—to make the present to build for the future that must be.

—Stephen Vincent Benét
(1898–1943)

CONCERNING Big Foot, Dim Sum, and Fat Farms. The rewards of seeing one's family word in print are relatively minor. Of course, there is a chance that once made public one or two of them might break through and become part of the language and belong to everyone. To be sure, the chance of this happening is slim. As John Moore wrote in his book, *You English Words,* "The odds against a new word surviving must be longer than those against a great oak-tree growing from any given acorn."

However, new words *are* coming along all the time, and they are not all jawbreakers from the world of science and technology. A case in point is a book published in 1987 that lists and defines the words that "have become firmly established in the language" in the previous twenty-six years. It is called *12,000 Words,* and anyone spending more than a few hours with it is likely to start thinking of pre-1961 America as a quaint place not that far removed from the world of Currier and Ives.

Imagine, if you can, an America without garage sales, hot tubs, slam dunks, dirt bikes, floppy disks, think tanks, Frisbees, Dumpsters, cursors, TV dinners, and cellulite. No way! (which, in case you haven't heard, is an "adv.—used interjectionally to express emphatic negation").

Hark back to a simpler and more innocent time when words like scuzzy and yucky did not exist, when people got the blues but not the blahs, and redeye was a medical condition, not a midnight flight. Those were the days when dozens of words—including chip, bunny, pot, adult, hardware, menu, character, and adult—meant something quite different than they do today.

Another way to look at all of this would be to imagine a modern Rip Van Winkle dozing off in 1961 and waking up today with a copy of *12,000 Words* at his side. He would have to come to terms with a dizzying array of shocks (culture and future), codes (genetic and zip), processors (food and word), effects (greenhouse and placebo), and theories (domino and big bang). Entries for walking catfish, black hole, gridlock, acid rain, and smart which would suggest that the whole thing was a work of fiction. He would doubtless dismiss the whole thing as absurd as discovering nouvelle cuisine, the designated hitter, big foot, and the fat farm.

The book *12,000 Words* is in fact a small dictionary published by Merriam-Webster as a supplement to *Webster's Third New International*, the gigantic unabridged dictionary published in 1961, which was, among other things, the year I turned twenty-one. It comes on the heels of *6,000 Words* (the first supplement brought out in 1976) and *9,000 Words* (1983), showing, if nothing else, the speed at which words enter the American language. The editors of *12,000*

Words are quick to point out that the words listed may have first appeared in English or been part of another language before 1961, but that they did not become *common* until after that date. For this reason, sushi is found here and so is nebbish.

As a compulsive compiler of lists, particularly word lists, I have been inspired by this book to create all sorts of new categories. Some are built on odd premises: Could I, for example, subsist on food defined and described since I voted in my first election? My post-1961 alphabetical buffet would include aioli, bananas foster, caldo verde, crudites, dim sum, dagwoods, empanadas, granola, green goddess dressing, havarti, junk food, kiwifruit, lane cake, nachos, peking duck, quiche lorraine, reuben sandwiches, steak diane, tabbouleh, vegeburgers, yakotori, and zuppa inglese. Along with the food itself come such essential food-related items as the doggy bag, salad bar, and wok. "The munchies" are here, and nosh is represented both as a noun and as a verb.

Another category suggested itself when I asked myself what kind of person could I invite to this feast. The list would, of course, be restricted to the types who emerged and got named in the last twenty-six years. Imagine a long buffet line peopled with yuppies, hippies, flower people, whistle-blowers, doves, hawks, grunts, hare krishnahs, empty nesters, nerds, hackers, non-persons, and teenyboppers. Despite their credentials, I would omit party poopers for the sake of the other guests. Speaking of people, there are a number of eponyms. Everybody knows about the Keogh plan named after Rep. Eugene James Keogh, and the Heimlich maneuver for surgeon Henry J. Heimlich, but more esoteric is the Chandler wobble—an oscillation of the earth's axis—named for astronomer Seth Carlo Chandler.

Other lists address those things that inspire new terms. For instance, humans still create "animalisms" like cold duck (cold turkey is a golden oldie), dog and pony show, cattle call, and pig out. The human body is a treasure trove for word coiners who have come up with the likes of knee-jerk, knuckle sandwich, and nose tackle.

Inanimate inspiration? There are more rock variations here —acid, folk-, glitter, hard, punk, soft—than you might expect to find in a medium-sized meadow (suggesting an answer to the age-old question posed by English teachers: "What's a meadow for?"). Like concentrated juice, we add water to some of our new words and phrases (watergate, waterfouling, and waterbed) and gild others (golden handshakes, oldies, and parachutes). The new English has a number of terms with numbers in them (PG-13, catch 22, top 40, uranium 238), including a few new terms using one (one-night stand, one-liner and one-on-one).

In the last few decades we have also done some pruning back to short terms (as in, "Take the limo to the deli and pick up some mayo"), and have even doubled up some short forms (sci-fi, sit-com, el-hi).

Is there a point to all of this compiling? The one I underscore with each new list is that it is not just the major societal and technical changes that help define and give texture to our lives, but the little ones as well.

Go back further and the changes become more dramatic. In *Our Times*, Mark Sullivan presented some of the words not yet in the dictionary in 1900. He listed hundreds of examples, but one sentence stands out: "There was no such word as rumrunner, nor hijacker, nor bolshevism, fundamentalism, behaviorism, Nordic, Freudian, complexes, ectoplasm, brain-storm, Rotary,

Kiwanis, blue-sky law, cafeteria, automat, sundae; nor mah-jongg, nor crossword puzzle."

English expands as things change, and there is nothing to prevent one's quirky family word from sliding into the mainstream. If such a thing ever happened to your family word, not only would it be deeply satisfying in the present, but it would also give a future generation of linguists a break, because they would know where it originated. Words like *kludge, raunchy, nerd,* and *humongous,* which started as family words, or words used in a small group, do not have points of origin, and for that reason they tend to drive linguists bonkers—along with the word *bonkers,* for that matter—because they don't offer standard explanations. I have often thought that *humongous* may have come from a playground or college campus, where one person might have said, "I have this humongous exam tomorrow and haven't even begun to study." It was repeated and repeated, and before long it was bouncing back and forth between both coasts and had even invaded Canada.

But if you still believe that it is all but impossible to claim title to a word, consider the following list, compiled from many sources but inspired and influenced by a similar and longer list in C. Merton Babcock's *Ordeal of American English.* It shows a word or a term, the first writer to use that word or term, and the date of that use. Some were deliberate coinages (such as those attributed to Gelett Burgess), while others may have been the result of no more than a writer with a keen ear who heard it from someone else.

agnostic	T.H. Huxley (who coined it because he was tired of being called an atheist)	1869
almighty dollar	Washington Irving	1836
Americana	Herman Melville	c.1886
belittle	Sinclair Lewis	1922
blurb	Gelett Burgess	1907
booboisie	H.L. Mencken	1922
brinksmanship	John Foster Dulles	1956
bromide	Gelett Burgess	1906
chairwoman	John Locke	1865
chortle	Lewis Carroll	1872
cold war	Walter Lippmann	1947
cybernetics	Norbert Weiner	1948
demoralize	Noah Webster	1794
ecdysiast (stripteaser)	H.L. Mencken	1940
egghead	Stewart Alsop	1942
galoot	Artemus Ward	1866
gamesmanship	Stephen Potter	1947
glad hand	George Ade	1896
honky-tonk	Carl Sandburg	1927
international	Jeremy Bentham	1790
ivory tower	Henry James	1917
lowbrow	Will Irwin	1905
milquetoast	H. T. Webster (after the Timid Soul, Casper Milquetoast)	1924
moola	John O'Hara	1939
motel	Architect Arthur S. Heineman	1924
multimillionaire	Oliver Wendell Holmes	1858
Okie	John Steinbeck	1939
panhandler	George Ade	1899
robot	Karel Capek	1923
side-kick	O'Henry	1904

socialite	*Time* magazine	1929
stuffed shirt	Willa Cather	1913
tightwad	George Ade	1900
timothy (grass)	Benjamin Franklin	1747
underground railway	Harriet Beecher Stowe	1852
whodunit	Donald Gordon	1930
workaholic	Pychologist Wayne E. Oates	1971
yankee	Johnathan Hastings	1713

Some individuals have actually brought a handful of new words into the language. As Robert Greenman points out in his *Words in Action,* some of the more notable word inventors included "John Milton (1608–1674): *impassive, earthshaking, lovelorn, pandemonium;* Sir Thomas More (1478–1535): *anticipate, exact, explain, fact, insinuate;* Sir Thomas Elyot (1490?–1546): *dedicate, maturity, protest, irritate;* and William Tyndale (1494?–1536): *beautiful* and *brokenhearted.*" Greenman also points out that Shakespeare created more than 1,500 words. He adds, "Some of them, true nonce words, never went further than their appearance in his plays, but others—like *bump, hurry, critical,* and *road*—are essential parts of our vocabulary today."

One more small list to drive home a point. This one was created as the by-product of a series of interviews I conducted at Merriam-Webster, Inc. in June of 1985. A year earlier the company had brought out its *Ninth New Collegiate Dictionary,* which had a fascinating new feature: words were identified as to the year in which they had first appeared in print—entered the language. In the wake of this dating, certain examples stood out in the minds of the editors for the simple reason that they were earlier—or later—than one might expect. I present them here to give an idea of the surprising debut dates of common words.

Astronaut—1926
Beef Wellington—1965
Bounty hunter—1957
Contact lens—1888
Electoral college—1691
Energize—1752
Granola—1971
Gunslinger—1951
Health food—1882, but "junk food" did not appear
    on the scene linguistically until 1971
Hot tub—1975
Marshmallow—pre-twelfth century
Murphy's law—1958
Politicize—1758
Sushi—1898
Verbalize—1609
Warmonger—1590
Zit—1961

CONCERNING Family Ways.

The family is one of nature's masterpieces.
                                        —George Santayana (1863–1952)

I love these family words because they are more than mere oddities. They are family traditions wrapped up in words. If any of you suspect that there will be a moment sometime in the future when I will shamelessly exploit the readers of this book by asking them for their favorite family words and customs to report in a sequel, you are correct. In fact, the time is now.

IMPORTANT ANNOUNCEMENT

I have collected these words for five years now, but it is clear that I have just scratched the surface and that there is more work to be done. There are many more words to be collected, as well as new areas to explore. Therefore, I hereby announce the beginning of a new collection, which I will call:

Family Ways

It will contain an even more motley assortment of things than the book you are now holding. For starters:

1. More family words in the vein of those in this book. Special attention will be paid, however, to terms that *must* exist somewhere in some family to describe a common phenomenon for which there is not an adequate mainstream word or expression. One correspondent, Kevin Bazzana of Kelowna, B.C., has found three words lacking. He suggests a search of the English-speaking world for

- A noun to describe the mistake one makes when telling the owner of a place that he acts as if "he owns the place."
- A noun to describe the inability of many foreigners to deal with the unstressed English vowel; hence *push* becomes *poosh.*

■ A verb to describe the ability to recall only the first line or title of any song (e.g., "Ramona la-da-da-da la-da-da-dee.")

There was another word that Bazzana found lacking, but he finally coined his own to fit the definition:

Sinorexia. The feeling of renewed hunger an hour after eating Chinese food.

2. Similes, metaphors, and other family expressions, on the order of

"Happy as a goat eating briars."
"That cut his water off" (*that put him in his place*)
"Got his tail in a crack" (*found himself in a bad position*)
"He leaves his steps so far behind" (*child observing long-legged man*)
"Cut me a sprout" (*give me a break*)

In a similar vein, a special place will be made for long-winded translations. One woman, Mary Beth McGowan, reported that her Italian grandmother could not say *colander*, so she called it "the pan that makes the water go and spaghetti stay." (This was "noodles stop, water go" in another family.)

3. Family gestures, signals, and other nonverbal forms of communication. I have several reports that a slight tug of the ear is a way of telling the rest of the family that it is time to go home.

4. Institutional family words. A 1986 letter on family words from David Saltman of "CBS News" mentioned that the CBS "family" had created a number of words, including these two:

Timmy. The word used to describe any particular expert who will be interviewed, as in "who can we get to be the timmy on that story?"

Goo-goos. The universal unit of currency for "CBS News" crews in foreign countries, as in "let me have a million goo-goos."

CBS is hardly alone in this regard, as was underscored by a December 29, 1987, article in *The Wall Street Journal* entitled "At Many Firms, Employees Speak A Language That's All Their Own." The article discussed such terms as *the great yellow father* (the Corporation itself at Eastman Kodak), *hipo* (IBMese for an employee with high potential), and *on the mouse* (descriptive of a lunch paid for by the company at Walt Disney World). More of these words and phrases beg to be collected from corporations, schools, government agencies, and other families in the larger sense.

However, what will most clearly distinguish *Family Ways* from this book will be its exploration of odd rituals and customs practiced within families and between friends. This was an idea first suggested by Jane Tesh of Mt. Airy, North Carolina, whose family has long been secretly passing small and strange objects back and forth. One of their current objects is a small, white cardboard tube. Ms. Tesh reports, "I left it in my sister's freezer in Iowa the last time I visited. She may not find it for months; then it's her turn to hide it."

The possibilities seem endless. Traditions for special days, like Valentine's Day, Halloween, and April Fool's Day, would seem like especially fertile ground. Some years ago, for example, a friend told me of his parents who had come to the United States from Italy and were about to observe their first Thanksgiving. Lacking full instructions for preparing a traditional turkey, they were stymied when it came time to fill the bird. The decision was then made to stuff it with ravioli. The tradition was created, and a second generation is now known for its pasta stuffing.

A few more examples of the kind of customs being sought:

Dumb Criminal Awards. A Milwaukee woman, Cate Pfeifer, reports an annual get-together during which she and some of her friends meet to crown the dumbest criminal of the year. All year long they keep their eyes out looking for candidates and meet shortly after the first of the year. Pfeifer's favorite winner was a man who had held up another man on the street and then discovered that the victim's wallet had no money in it. The holdup man apparently began feeling sorry for the other man, got in his car and found him. He threw the wallet out of the car window and sped off, not realizing that he had thrown his own wallet—replete with identification—at the feet of his victim.

The 109-Year-Old Fruitcake. A number of families have fruitcakes that have survived for several holiday seasons. It is also no secret that these heavy, boozy desserts are not everybody's piece of cake, and one given as a gift often gets rewrapped and given out to someone else. This prompted Johnny Carson to conclude that there is only one fruitcake in the world and to get *New York Times* columnist Russell Baker to write about his ancient fruitcake, baked by Miles Standish and later left to him in his Great Uncle Elmer's will.

A few days after Christmas in 1986 the Associated Press carried a wire story on what is probably the ultimate in family fruitcake tradition. Under a Tecumseh, Michigan, dateline, the story began "When Fridelia Ford died in 1879, she left behind an edible heirloom that has been kept in the family for more than a century." It seems that the woman who had created the cake planned to allow it to age for a year, but she died before the year was up. It was decided to preserve it in her honor, and over the years various members of the family have acted as the cake's official guardian.

It goes without saying that family traditions are important; yet they may be even more important than we tend to think. It a 1987 Washington *Post* article on family traditions, Brett Williams, associate professor of anthropology and American studies at American University, is quoted on studies examining families with disturbed children. Williams says that "these families didn't seem to set aside anything as special. They didn't try to build traditions. Mealtimes were mundane. Bedtimes were boring. Leaving the house and coming back was completely without spirit. The absence of traditions and rituals in these families was giving the children the message that they weren't important and that the family wasn't important."

It would also seem that the time is right for a celebration of private family traditions. Perhaps this is just the voice of middle age, but it seems that public traditions are taking it on the chin. We now celebrate something called President's Day, bring movies home in plastic bags, and live in subdivisions without sidewalks. The sociability of the front porch is giving way to the privacy of the deck. A previous generation's dirt and pavement games—marbles, hop-scotch, jacks, stickball, jump rope—seem to have been co-opted by highly supervised leagues run by several layers of adult hierarchy or reduced to a series of competing blips on a computer screen.

So, send up three cheers for the traditions we establish with family and friends and report them to this collector of family words, phrases, coinages, rituals, verbal antiques, and quality phlurrg, who can be reached at P.O. Box 80, Garrett Park, MD 20896-0080.

Acknowledgments

Here, in one place, are the names of a number of the people who donated their family words to this little dictionary. I am indebted to them, and to the many anonymous callers to talk shows on the following radio stations:

CFOS	Owen Sound, Ontario	WHO	Des Moines, Iowa
CFQC	Saskatoon	WIND	Chicago
KARN	Little Rock	WIOD	Miami, Florida
KGO	San Francisco	WKIS	Orlando, Florida
KMOX	St. Louis	WMCA	New York
KNBR	San Francisco	WNYC	New York
KSUN	Phoenix	WPLP	Pinellas Park, Florida
KTRH	Houston		
WAMU	Washington, D.C.	WRC	Washington, D.C.
WCKY	Cincinnati	WWD	Philadelphia
WFD	Flint, Michigan	WXYZ	Detroit
WHDH	Boston	Minnesota Public Radio	
WHJJ	Providence, Rhode Island		

The individuals who contributed to the project:

Reinhold A. Aman
William Amatruda
Jay Ames
Carol Andresen
Lois S. Appel

Marlene Aronow
Russell Ash
Donald W. Athearn
Margaret Atwood
Susan Austin

Patricia J. Axline
Joseph Badger
Sharman Badgett
M. Baeb
Maryjane Bailey
Marchall T. Baker
Rachel Barenblat
Maureen Barnard
Anne Barnes
The Barouch family
Tracy Barrett
Christopher Barth
Ruth Bauerle
Kevin Bazzana
Mrs. William Bendel
Anna Berg
Walter Berkov
Deborah Bigelow
Soo Bishop
Terence Blacker
Toni Blair
Sylvia Blowers
Laura Bobbitt
Betrenia Bowker
Evelyn M. Bowles
Harrison Boyle
Dorothy Lia Braaten
Jon Bracker
Larry Broadmore
Lynne Bronstein
Catherine Brooks
Erica Brothers
Barbara Brown
Marilyn Brown
Martin M. Bruce
Sally L. Brune

Frank Brusca
Caroline Bryan
Monica E. Buergler
Christi Burchyns
Catherine Burns
Jeremy Burr
Carol Buss
Judith Cadigan
Barbara Calures
Cleo S. Carey
Alan and Michele
    Carpenter
Dave Carr
Carole L. Carrick
Gregory J. Cebelak
Frank Celentano
Tammy Chadbourne
Robert G. Chamberlain
Howard Channing
Phillip Chaplin
Carolyn Chappell
Renee Charles
Robert Chirico
Cathy M. Clark
John Clark
Lynn Clark
Paul B. Clifford
S. Clemens
Tracy Cobbs
Judith Sara Cohen
Lena Cole
William Rossa Cole
Kate Contos
Bertram C. Cooper
John Corcoran
Teresa Cornelius

Gillian and Steve Crabtree
Roger Crabtree
Diana Gilbert Craft
Nancy Craig
Janet W. Crampton
Sue Crawford
Jean Scott Creighton
Virginia and Bill Cressey
Don Crinklaw
Neil Croll
Louise Crowder
Karen Cukrowski
Amy Culver
Ann Cuniff
Diane Curtis
Norinne Hilchey Daly
Kevin Dammen
Norma Daniel
Edie Danieli
David Dattie
Dr. Charles Davies
Sally O. Davis
Alice L. Deal
S. Percy Dean
Gene Deitch
Nita Denny
Bill Denton
Wilma P. Derting
Peter DeWeese
C. Dick
James Dierken
Carole A. Digel
Alicia DiRado
Michele Newton Dohse
Faye Donaghey

Nancy Dotson
Margaret Drye
John Duffie
Russel J. Dunn, Sr.
Mary Eccher
Russell Edgerton
Debra Elkins
V. Elrod
Bryan R. Embrey
Kathy Enders
George Englebretsen
Nona West Eudy
Joanne Evans
Susan Jordan Everton
Robert Falk
Ian Farber
Jon Fasman
Patricia Fay
Karen Feinberg
Steve Fergenbaum
K.L.F. Findell
J.L. Fosse
Jan Franklin
Lisa E. Freedman
Rebecca Rasor Freeman
Shari Gackstatter
Michael P. Gagnon
Ellen Gald
Martin Gardner
Sher Bird Garfield
Barbara Gerovac
Walt Giachini
Beverly Giancola
Nel Gibbs
Barbara Gilfillen
Frederic W. Gill

Tom Gill
Kay Gleason
Mark Gloor
Sally Godfrey
Patricia Goff
Morton Goldberg
E. Goodman
John Gormley
Joseph C. Goulden
Sharon Grace
Carolyn Gray
Eric Greb
Esther S. Gross
Gayle Grove
Lynne Gucwa
Heidi Gustafson
Stephen Haase
Elaine Herson Hadley
Kim Haglund
The Hague family
Linda Halloin
Johnathan R. Hancock
Nelson Hanke
Leslie Hanscom
Barb Hanselman
Donna Hargrave
Tamara L. Harless
James H. Harms
Sharon A. Harris
Jane Harrison
Mike Hartnett
Barbara Hasty
Kathleen R. Hayes
John G. Hedemann
Marlene Heinen
Wendy Heldke

Pam Herman
Lory Hess
Robert P. Hesse
Robert D. Higginbotham
Anne Higgins
Tammy S. Hill
Jane and Paul Hinckley
Dawn Hogarth
Eve. C. Holberg
Nan Holland
Jan Holloway
Libby Holmes
Janet W. Hook
Verna Horning
Claire Howard
Colin Howard
Kellie L. Huggler
Judith Ann Hughes
Madeline Hutchinson
Geof Huth
Arnold Isaacs
Lisa Simon Jablon
Adrian B. James
Libby James
Elaine Jares
Janet Jirouschek
Warren and Bobby
   Johnston
Jon B. Jolly
Candy Jones
Christina Jones
Tia Karelson
Stewart Kauffman
Michael Kaye
Kathleen Keefe
Peggy Keller

Lynn Kelley
Linda Kent
Sandra M.S. Kent
Eloise C. Kern
Mindy Kettner
Sue King
Ruth Kingsley
Donna Kipp
George Kirby
Geri Kirkpatrick
Chet Klingensmith
Sally P. Knight
Julie Knippling
Mavis Koehler
Audrey Konwiser
Martin S. Kottmeyer
Bobby Kraft
Abbe Krissman
Joyce Reynolds Kurth
Bonnie Kurtz
Karen Lane
M.A. Lange
Gwynne A. Laning
Tara Lawson
Richard Lederer
Anna Lee
Joanne Lee
Marion Lehuta
Jessie Levine
Tobey Levine
Fred Levy
Dorothy LiaBraaten
Marjorie Linhares
Mary Little
Anita Locke
Enok Lohne

Cynthia MacGregor
Tom MacGregor
Gary MacSahra
John A. Main
Tamarah Malley
Janet Mangalvedhe
Peg Manion
Norman Mark
Barbara Markunas
Catherine Marshall
Dorothy J. Martin
Ivan Martin
Stephen V. Masse
Edward Mayo
Rhonda and Tom
    McCarty
Mary Beth McGowan
Dan McKenney
Donna McLaughlin
Heather McMaster
Susan McVey
Richard Mende
Lisa Meredith
Timothy B. Messick
Jim and Jule Michelini
Deb Miller
Susan Mills
Diana Montague
Vickie Moreland
Jennifer Morrison
Sue Mosher
Eileen Mozingo
David Mumper
Suzie Mundeu
Patti Murphy
Raymond J. Nelson

Nancy Nemec
Vickie Nesbit
Sylvia Anthony Newman
Elmer S. Newman
Scott Newsome
LynnErna Niebergall
Jean M. Ogden
Frank O'Hara
Carol Ohlson
Debbie Paliagas
Herbert Paper
Allison Parker-Hedrick
Virginia Pastoor
Myra Patner
Naomi Patterson
Julie Paull
George Pelletieri
Judy Pemberton
Grace H. Perkins
Doris L. Pertz
Mr. and Mrs. Mark
   Petersen.
Cate Pfeifer
Gerald M. Phillips
Susan Pinto
Charles D. Poe
Mrs. Thomas Polek
Jerald D. Pope
Philip N. Price
Robert Prokop
Janet Pugh
Dale and Barbara Pullen
Kathleen Quastler
Jane Quinn
Suzie Radus

Ann Raimond
Maxine Rapoport
Michael Ray
Allen Walker Read
Ross Reader
Sherry Reardon
Diane Rehm
Penny Richards
Garrett Riggs
Florence J. Ring
Joyce Rizzo
Mary M. Roberts
Randy Roberts
Ursula Roberts
Jack P. Roe
Mary Rogers
The Roussos family
David Saltman
David Andrew Saltzman
Elizabeth Samuels
Wanda Sanborn
Martha Sandman
Roberta Sandrin
Elyce K.D. Santerre
Shirley Sax
Linda Schaub
Lori Schlichtori
Vicki Schooler
Jeanne Schrieber
Jerrold B. Schwartz
Margaret Schweitzer
Margo B. Schworm
Dallas Shaffer
Richard Shanks
Leila Shapiro

Mildred Shapiro
Becky Sharp
Christine M. Short
Daniel and Matthew
   Sissman
Karen Sjolund
Nancy Skewis
Betty Skinner
Bob and Monika Skole
Forrest Slavens
P.F. Smith
Stephen E. Smith
Jean E. Smythe
Peg Snyder
Patricia Spaeth
Ed Spingarn
Joel M. Spivak
Tina Stano
Ashley H. Steele
Debbie Steensland
David Stewart
Nancy Stewart
Doug Stip
Jean Stockton
W. Bryan Stout
William Tammeus
Elsie Tanka
Mary J. Tanner
Stacy Tatman
Mrs. Fred Terry
Jane Tesh
Rich Tewell
Elisabeth S. Thacher
Barbara Thompson
Faith M. Thompson

Judy Thompson
Steven Thomson
James and Diantha
   Thorpe
Christine H. Tiffany
J.G. Timm
Arlene Tishe
Dorothy E. Tomkins
Dorothy Topping
Johnathan Tourtellot
Laurie Travis
Edwin Tribble
Lillian Tudiver
Jane Tukey
Donna Turner
Joe Turner
Fran Urban
Andrea Veri
Felicia Volkman
Cathy Voss
Todd W. Wallingen
Vicki Ward
Kelly L. Webb
D. Weber
Ruth R. Wedge
Kenneth P. Weinkauf
Stephen Wells
Bob and Mary West
Jean Wheatley
Bob Wheeler
Frank Whitby
Sally White
George and Ruth Whitin
Brad Whitlock
Bill H. Whitton

Neal Wilgus
Ann Marie Willer
Al Williams
Meredith G. Williams
Ben Willis
Julia F. Wilson
Lisa Wilson
Mike Wilson
Donald R. Wing
Carolin Winslow
Polly Winter

Doris P. Wipert
Jeanne Witmer
Lee M. Wrenn
The Woskoff family
Clayton W. Yoho
Arlene Yolles
Mary Young
Joanne Zall
Jeanne Zieman
Rick Zimmerman
Ann Zlamal

Special added thanks to Nancy Dickson, the late John A. Main, Richard Lederer, Charles F. Dery and Warren and Bobby Johnston for their extraordinary help. Their influence is felt on almost every page.

Bibliography

American Speech, Biography of the Word "Insinuendo," February 1934.

Asbell, Bernard, The Little World of Orville K. Snav. *Playboy,* April 1958.

Atlantic Monthly, Improvised Words. November 1908.

Babcock, C. Merton, *The Ordeal of American English.* Houghton Mifflin, Boston, 1968.

Barlough, J. Ernest, *The Archaicon.* Scarecrow Press, Metuchen, N.J., 1974.

Baum, Joan, Doing "the Scotton." *Christian Science Monitor,* June 2, 1983.

Bellow, Saul, *Humboldt's Gift.* Viking, New York, 1975.

Berkov, Walter, Editor's Report column in the Cleveland *Plain Dealer.* April 14, 21, 28, May 5, 12, 19, 1985.

Blake, Norman, *Non-Standard Language in English Literature.* Andre Deutsch, London, 1981.

Bombeck, Erma, Mother Makes Decision Puts FHB Plan in Action. *At Wit's End* column in the *Rocky Mountain Telegram,* April 2, 1985.

Breathnach, Sarah Ban, Tradition, the Tie That Defines. Washington *Post,* March 3, 1987.

Brook, G.L., *Varieties of English.* Macmillan, London, 1973.

Brown, Ivor, *I Give You My Word.* Dutton, New York, 1948.

Ciardi, John, *Good Words to You.* Harper & Row, New York, 1987.

Cornog, Martha, Genital Pet Names: Regularities in "Personal" Naming Behavior. Paper presented at the annual meeting of the American Anthropological Association in Washington, D.C., December 4–7, 1982.

Dickens, Charles, *David Copperfield.* Dodd, Mead, New York, 1943. (Great Illustrated Classics Edition).

Dickson, Paul, All in the Family. *Games,* June 1986.

Duffie, John, Talking in the Family Way. *Monday Magazine,* Victoria, B.C., April 9, 1982.

———, The British to the Rescue. *Monday Magazine,* Victoria, B.C., May 21, 1982.

Eisen, Jack, Neighbors Cry NIMBY. *Metro Scene* column in the *Washington Post,* February 13, 1983.

Feinstein, John, Cremins Uneasy as the "Overdog." *Washington Post,* December 28, 1984.

Funk, Charles Earle, *Heavens to Betsy! And Other Curious Sayings.* Harper and Brothers, New York, 1955.

Garrett, Kim S., Family Stories and Sayings. In *Singers and Storytellers* (Publications of the Texas Folklore Society) 30, 1961

Garvey, John, When Words Go Private. *Commonweal,* February 10, 1984.

Goldstein, Marilyn, Ummm's the Word—For Now. *Newsday,* August 31, 1986.

Gordon, Ian Being Beezled. *The Listener* (New Zealand), December 18, 1982.

Greene, Amsel, *Pullet Surprises.* Scott, Foresman, Glenview, Ill., 1969.

Greenman, Robert, *Words in Action.* Times Books, New York, 1983.

Hall, Rich, and friends, *Sniglets.* Collier Books, New York, 1984.

Herzberg, Max J., Who Makes Up the New Words? *Word Study,* October 1948.

Holt, Alfred H., *Phrase and Word Origins.* Dover Books, New York, 1961.

Jesperson, Otto, *Language: Its Nature, Development and Origin.* Allen & Unwin, London, 1923, pp. 161–188.

Kendal, Robert, People, Prizes, Places. *Competitors Journal,* August 8, 1985.

Keyes, Ralph, Family Spoken Here. *Good Housekeeping,* April 1986.

Lederer, Richard, All in the Family. *The Concord Monitor* October 9, 1985.

————, Some More Words from the Family. *Concord Monitor,* November 11, 1985.

Levitt, John and Joan, *The Spell of Words.* Darwen Finlayson, London, 1959.

McReynolds, Helen Jarvis, Some Straight Talk on "Boomerangs." *New York Times,* May 15, 1983.

Macalister, R.A. Stewart, *The Secret Languages of Ireland.* Cambridge University Press, Cambridge, England, 1937.

Macy, William F., *The Nantucket Scrap Basket.* Houghton Mifflin, Boston, 1930.

May, John Allan, Then There's Smizzle and Droggle. *Christian Science Monitor,* December 1, 1953.

Miller, Michael W., At Many Firms, Employees Speak a Language That's All Their Own. *The Wall Street Journal,* December 29, 1987.

Milne, A.A., Christmas Party. In *A Table Near the Band and Other Stories.* Methuen, London, 1950.

Moore, John, *You English Words.* Collins, London, 1961.

New Yorker, Recaptoids. October 3, 1983.

Opie, Iona and Peter, *The Lore and Language of Schoolchildren.* Oxford University Press, London, 1959.

Partridge, Eric, *Slang Today and Yesterday,* Third Edition; Macmillan, New York 1950.

Read, Allen Walker, Family Words in English. *American Speech,* February 1962.

Richman; Phyllis C., Presidential Mystery Recipe. *Washington Post,* July 3, 1983

Sandburg, Carl, *Prairie Town Boy.* Harcourt, Brace, New York, 1955.

Sherk, Bill, *Brave New Words.* Doubleday Canada Ltd., Toronto, 1979.

————, *500 Years of New Words.* Doubleday, New York, 1983.

————, *More Brave New Words.* Doubleday Canada Ltd. Toronto, 1981

Soukhanov, Anne H., Word Watch. *The Atlantic,* June 1987.

Spiegl, Fritz, Endpiece. *The Listener,* (New Zealand) April
4, 1985.

Swetnam, George, The Great Khulyages Conspiracy.
Pittsburgh Press, March 14, 1971.

Tribble, Edwin, ed., *A Chime of Words: The Letters of
Logan Pearsall Smith.* Ticknor and Fields, New York,
1984.

Van Buren, Abigail, Let's Consider the Subject Closed.
Her Universal Press Syndicate column for July 22,
1986.

Woman's Day. A Few Words About Words. August 1963.

Worth, Fred L., *The Complete Unabridged Super Trivia
Encyclopedia.* Brooke House, Los Angeles, 1977.

Zeitlin, Steven J., Kotkin, Amy J., and Baker, Holly
Cutting, *A Celebration of American Folklore:*
Pantheon, New York, 1982.